THE TASTE OF OUR TIME

Collection planned and directed by

ALBERT SKIRA

BIOGRAPHICAL AND CRITICAL STUDY

BY

PAUL GUINARD

Translated by James Emmons

"EL GRECO"

SKIRA

Title page: St Luke (detail), c. 1605-1610.
Library of Congress Catalog Card Number: 56-7923.

★

Distributed in the United States by
THE WORLD PUBLISHING COMPANY
2231 West 110th Street - Cleveland 2, Ohio.

In the past half-century everything has been said that could be said about El Greco. Yet on many essential points we are none the wiser. Who was El Greco? Why did he paint as he did? How is it that this Greek schooled in Italy came to settle in Spain, at Toledo? And there, after the masterpieces of his maturity, in which the Golden Age of Spain saw the best of its piety mirrored, how did he come to create the stark and supernatural art of his old age? We shall never know, and we may as well resign ourselves to never knowing. In view of the paucity of firsthand information and, above all, the loss of those mysterious treatises on painting and architecture attributed to El Greco by early biographers, we must content ourselves with more or less ingenious speculations and interpretations, none of which add a particle of certainty to what we really know about the artist. It has proved no more rewarding to look to El Greco for the "secret of Toledo" than to look to Toledo for the "secret of El Greco." The most elementary facts about his life and the genesis of his pictures (often signed, rarely dated) are largely wanting, nor is it reasonable to hope for many more lost pictures or documents to come to light. Fortunately the fruit of the great renewal of interest felt in El Greco has been a vast increase in our knowledge of him now as compared with what it was in the 19th century. There is admittedly a negative side—a host of fakes and dubious attributions having found their way into so-called "complete" catalogues—but on the whole a great forward stride has been made. Problems of chronology, of source material, of influences exerted on and by El Greco, have been solved or accurately localized. It is true that Cossío's monumental biography of El Greco, the very first, published in 1908, has lost none of its critical solidity and its freshness. But we can readily measure the ground covered since then by comparing it with such recent works as that of J. Camón Aznar, a veritable summa *of the available knowledge of El Greco and his art. One of the aims of this book will be that of summing up the positive results of previous research-work, approaching the subject analytically rather than synthetically; we shall be concerned with isolating the problems that remain unsolved and with carefully distinguishing between hypotheses, however clever or tempting, and the known facts. No speculations or lyricism here then, but a strictly matter-of-fact approach which, it is hoped, will provide the reader with a useful introduction to El Greco.*

BIOGRAPHICAL SUMMARY

1541 Birth of El Greco (Domenikos Theotokopoulos) at Candia, Crete.

C. 1560-1570 Lives and works in or around Venice, in the entourage of Titian, Jacopo Bassano and Tintoretto.

    1563 Work begins on the convent of the Escorial, founded by King Philip II of Spain.

    1564 Death of Michelangelo in Rome.

1570 El Greco goes to Rome where he is introduced at the Farnese Palace by Giulio Clovio, the miniature-painter.

1570-1575 (?) Lives and works in Rome.

    1571 Battle of Lepanto in which the combined naval forces of Venice and Spain defeat the Turks.

    1575 Work begins on the church of the Escorial.

1576 El Greco goes to Madrid.

1576-1577 El Greco arrives in Toledo and is commissioned to paint altarpieces for the church of Santo Domingo el Antiguo and the ''Espolio'' for the Cathedral.

1578 Birth of Jorge Manuel, son of El Greco and Doña Jerónima de las Cuevas.

1579 The high price charged for the ''Espolio'' involves him in a lawsuit.

1580 King Philip II commissions El Greco to paint ''The Martyrdom of St Maurice'' for the Escorial and orders the prior of the convent to supply him with fine-ground colors for the work.

1582 El Greco called in to serve as interpreter at the hearing of a Greek, Michael Rizo, before the Inquisition of Toledo.

1583 Payment made El Greco for ''The Martyrdom of St Maurice'' (800 ducats).

1584 The "St Maurice" is duly received by the king and transmitted to the prior of the convent of the Escorial, but it is not hung in its destined place in the church, another picture being ordered instead from the Italian painter Romulo Cincinnati.

1585 El Greco rents a suite of twenty-four rooms in the palace of the Marquis of Villena.

1586 Signs the contract for "The Burial of Count Orgaz" for the church of Santo Tomé in Toledo and finishes the picture the same year.

1588 El Greco sues the parish of Santo Tomé for payment of "The Burial of Count Orgaz" and wins his case.

1591 Altarpiece for the church of Talavera la Vieja in Estremadura.

1596 The Council of Castile orders an altarpiece from him for the College of Doña María de Aragón in Madrid.

1597 Commissioned to paint altarpieces for the Capilla de San José, Toledo. Contacts with dealers at Seville and Genoa for the export of his pictures.

1598 Death of Philip II, succeeded by his son Philip III.

1599 Birth of Velazquez in Seville.

1600 Finishes the altarpiece for the College of Doña María de Aragón, Madrid. Lodges in the house of Don Juan Suárez de Toledo.

1603 Commissioned to paint a "St Bernardin of Siena" for the chapel of the San Bernardino College, Toledo.
Signs a contract for paintings for the Hospice of the Caridad at Illescas, midway between Toledo and Madrid.

1604 Moves back to his vast suite of rooms in the palace of the Marquis of Villena.
Birth of Gabriel, only son of Jorge Manuel Theotokopoulos by his first wife Alfonsa de los Morales (the boy became an Augustinian monk in 1622 under his mother's name).
Death of Manusos Theotokopoulos, a relative (perhaps a brother) of El Greco, with whom he was living.

1605-1607 Protracted lawsuit over payment of the Illescas altarpieces.

1607 Commissioned by the municipal authorities of Toledo to do paintings for the Oballe Chapel in the church of San Vicente.

1608 Signs a contract with the Hospice of San Juan Bautista (also known as the Tavera Hospice) for several altarpieces (which he was never to complete).

1609 Expulsion of the Moors from Spain by order of Philip III.

1611 Commissioned by the municipality of Toledo to make a cenotaph for the memorial service in Toledo Cathedral in honor of Queen Margaret. Receives a visit from Francisco Pacheco, the painter and art-historian (later the master and father-in-law of Velazquez).

1614 March 31. Too weak to draw up his will, El Greco puts all his affairs in the hands of his son Jorge Manuel.
April 7. Death of El Greco, buried in Santo Domingo el Antiguo.

1617 Death of Alfonsa de los Morales, wife of Jorge Manuel.

1619 El Greco's remains are transferred from Santo Domingo to San Torcuato.

1625 Appointed "master of works" at Toledo Cathedral, Jorge Manuel supervises rebuilding of the Mozarabic Chapel.

1631 Death of Jorge Manuel.

EL GRECO IN HIS OWN TIME

CORONATION OF A SAINT OR KING (MODENA POLYPTYCH), BEFORE 1570.

FROM CRETE TO TOLEDO

E L GRECO lived to be seventy-three years old. Thanks to the painstaking research-work of San Román in the archives of Toledo, the latter half of his career has become almost familiar to us. The earlier half, however, is a complete blank except for three isolated dates. In 1541 Domenikos Theotokopoulos was born at Candia, capital of Venetian Crete. In November 1570 the "young Candiot, pupil of Titian," was welcomed to Rome by Giulio Clovio who, numbering him among "the most excellent in painting," sollicited Cardinal Farnese to house him temporarily in the garret of his palace. In July 1577 "Mecer Dominico Theotocopuli" (bringing with him his Italian nickname of "Il Greco," soon hispanicized to "El Greco") appeared in Toledo after a sojourn in Madrid.

The rest is mere conjecture. We know next to nothing about his family: his ancestors migrated from Constantinople to Crete in the 14th century and, as they were landowners in the island, must have been fairly well-to-do. We know nothing about his religious upbringing: was he born a Catholic or converted later in life? We know nothing about his training as a painter: perhaps he was schooled in the Cretan monasteries, perhaps in the studios of the Greco-Venetian "madonneri" on the Rialto in Venice, who can say? Impossible to ascertain the date of his arrival in Venice, doubtless prior to 1560 as he must have been very young. Impossible to glean a single clue to his presumable apprenticeship at Bassano in the studio of Jacopo da Ponte, his possible share in the last works of Titian, his conjectured stays at Reggio Emilia, Parma and Siena, or the conjectured second stay at Venice after he had left Rome. No documentary evidence has ever been produced in support of any of these theories which various critics have advanced—and others contradicted—in the past half-century.

The situation is the same as concerns the chronology of his works. The catalogue of paintings ascribed to his Italian period has "mushroomed" to alarming proportions. Even the most generally accepted of his early works, though signed in Greek characters, never bear a date. If we accept the *Descent from the Cross* (Venice) and the *Adoration of the Shepherds* (Bergamo) recently published by Pallucchini, together with the dates of 1565 for the first and 1567 for the second, then the El Greco of this period appears as a clever but unoriginal potboiler of current Venetian and Roman styles crossed with elements lifted from Italian and Flemish prints. Since we have no established facts to go on, it is only logical to suppose that he progressed from the style of a Greco-Venetian artisan to the style of a Veneto-Roman painter; that he began with the small wooden panels typical of that age and milieu, painted in tempera in bright, acid tones (the most significant example being the portable polyptych signed "Domenikos" which Pallucchini discovered in the attic of the Galleria Estense in Modena in 1937 and which, alongside the most obvious borrowings from the Byzantine style, offers the first version of several subjects to which El Greco reverted in later years); that he moved on to Titianesque oil paintings, brightly colored and rich in architectural details and accessories (e.g. *The Healing of the Blind Man* at Dresden and *Christ driving the Traders from the Temple* in the Minneapolis Museum of Art); and that thereafter, often with the same themes, he achieved a more concentrated expression and a greater vigor of form (e.g. *The Healing of the Blind Man* at Parma, *Christ driving the Traders from the Temple* in the National Gallery, London, the *Portrait of Giulio Clovio* in the Naples Pinacoteca, the *Portrait of Vincentio Anastagi* in the Frick Collection, and the small *Pietà* from the Johnson Collection at the Philadelphia Museum of Art). But did his art really evolve with such mathematical regularity? Very possibly it did not.

At any rate the dating of his works is still a matter of much debate; as far as many pictures are concerned, one guess is as good as another.

The most tantalizing problem of all is this: why and in what circumstances did El Greco go to Spain? He haughtily declined to give an answer when, in the course of one of the many lawsuits in which he was involved, this question was put to him pointblank. According to Mancini, private physician to Pope Urban VIII, writing early in the 17th century, El Greco received at Rome as many commissions as he could handle and even had a pupil, Lattantio Bonastri; but his disobliging comments on Michelangelo turned the entire Roman art world against him and he was finally forced to fly the city. Arrogant and uncompromising, proudly aware of his own merits and originality amidst an army of rank imitators, El Greco must have given offense more than once. Even so, the ill-will of his fellow artists hardly accounts for his emigrating to Spain. The years 1570-1575 saw the completion of the Escorial, with Philip II bringing together the team of artists who were to carry out the work of decoration. Concurrently the Farnese Palace was the meeting-place of all Spanish humanists living in Rome, and through the librarian there, Canon Fulvio Orsini, early friend and patron of El Greco and a keen collector of antiques, medallions and paintings, he no doubt came into contact with them. Perhaps it had already struck him that Spain, future Eldorado of painters from all over Europe, had much to offer under a monarch who was not only the victor of Lepanto but one of the most enlightened patrons of Titian. In any case he had every opportunity to meet such Spaniards as the Greek scholar Pedro Chacón and the Dean of Cuenca Cathedral Don Luis de Castilla (later one of his most loyal friends and the executor of his will) and they might have urged him to seek his fortune in Spain and promised him an introduction at Court.

GREAT EXPECTATIONS

With his arrival at Toledo we begin to get a clearer picture of things. His first seven years there sealed his destiny. He went on record as declaring that neither family ties nor material interests had brought him to Toledo, but he had not been there long before he had formed a lasting tie, a son, Jorge Manuel, being born to him in 1578. Whether or not the mother of the child, Doña Jerónima de las Cuevas, was his lawful wife or his mistress is an enigma over which too much ink has been spilt already. No extant document refers to her as his wife. Plain common sense, however, argues strongly in favor of marriage as against concubinage. The Spanish title of courtesy "Doña" which precedes every known mention of her name implies noble birth. That a concubine of her rank should be referred to openly in notarized deeds and writs drawn up in 16th-century Toledo seems extremely unlikely.

In any event the wandering Greek settled for good in Toledo where he found in Doña Jerónima a loyal, lifelong helpmate and a source of inspiration who, in his eyes, doubtless embodied the ideal of womanhood that every creative artist yearns for. Is she the famous *Woman with a Fur* in the Stirling-Maxwell Collection at Glasgow? It is tempting to think so, but there is still a broad division of opinion as to whether this portrait is really by El Greco. The fact remains that the face of a single woman is common to the first masterpieces of the Toledo period, a long, oval-shaped face with large, tender, sorrowful eyes; this is the woman who looks out of his pictures almost obsessively right up to his death. It is only natural that this should be Jerónima; she, presumably, is Mary Magdalen in the *Espolio* and the *Veronica* from the church of Santo Domingo el Antiguo, now preserved in the collection of Doña María Luisa Caturla in Madrid.

ADORATION OF THE NAME OF JESUS (DREAM OF PHILIP II), C. 1580.

Two large commissions took up most of his time from 1577 to 1579. Probably he owed them both to the Dean of the Cathedral, Don Diego de Castilla, elder brother of Don Luis de Castilla whom he had met in Rome. The Cistercian convent of Santo Domingo el Antiguo had been rebuilt in 1575 to the plans of Juan Herrera, the architect who completed the Escorial. El Greco was commissioned to paint the altarpieces, for which he also designed allegorical figures of the seven Virtues, executed by the sculptor Juan Bautista Monegro. The convent and its austere church remain intact to this day in one of the highest, most solitary and commanding spots in Toledo. Unfortunately the main altar has been mutilated: the central panel, *The Assumption of the Virgin*, is now in the Art Institute of Chicago; *The Trinity* and *St Benedict* are in the Prado; the pendant of the latter, *St Bernard*, found its way into the Chéramy Collection, Paris. The two *SS John*, the *Holy Face* and the side altars (an *Adoration of the Shepherds* with, above, *St Jerome* and *The Resurrection*) still give a good idea of this magnificent set of works. Something of a "homage" to the Italian art he had learned in his youth, this is also a farewell to it; a certain stark vigor and cold brilliance strike a new note, that of a master in his own right.

Another great work of this period, commissioned for the cathedral, holds even more promise for the future. Lifted from the altarpiece El Greco himself designed for it (now lost, all that remains being a small figure group carved in wood), this *Espolio* (i.e. a picture of Christ being insulted before being despoiled of His tunic) still lights up the somber sacristy of Toledo Cathedral. The novelty of the theme, the vividness of the broad purple tunic amid the throng of centurions with their steely armor breastplates and helmets, the majestic calm of the figure of Christ—all this made a direct appeal to the people. And though the orthodox-minded theologians in authority made

THE HOLY WOMEN, DETAIL OF THE ESPOLIO, 1579.

JORGE MANUEL, DETAIL OF THE BURIAL OF COUNT ORGAZ, 1586.

war on him for including the three Marys (the Gospels making no explicit mention of their presence at this stage of the Passion), and though under the threat of imprisonment he pledged himself to modify the work accordingly, it has somehow come down to us unchanged. What is more, out of some fourteen small-size replicas and variants he made of this picture, only four have come through without the figures in question.

For El Greco these early successes were but the means to a more important end: the king's patronage. He now began angling for royal favor with, it would seem, the strange little panel in the Escorial long known as *The Dream of Philip II* (now correctly titled as an *Adoration of the Name of Jesus*), which may be considered either as a spontaneous act of homage to the reigning monarch or as a trial picture set to test the powers of an aspirant. The apparent age of the king, seen kneeling in the foreground on the right, makes either of these hypotheses more likely than Cossío's late dating of the picture. In 1580 came the stroke of fortune El Greco had been waiting for: a royal order for a large-scale picture, *The Martyrdom of St Maurice*, for one of the chapels of the Escorial. But its completion four years later marked a critical juncture in El Greco's career. With his classical turn of mind, and accustomed as he was to the warm tones of Titian, Philip II was taken aback by this immense painting all in acid blues and yellows, this "invitation to death" (as the late José Ortega y Gasset once described it) in which the colloquy in progress between five or six warriors, shown hugely aloof and motionless in the foreground, completely overshadows the ordeal of St Maurice and the extermination of the Theban Legion which is actually the theme of the picture. The king scrupulously paid for the work but did not have it hung in its destined place and ordered another instead from the Italian painter Romulo Cincinnati. This was a cruel blow to El Greco's pride and brought his ambitions to nothing.

A NEW LIFE IN TOLEDO

EL GRECO abandoned his ambitions for a place in the sun at Court and resigned himself to local celebrity in Toledo. Rising sharply on a rugged hilltop above the river Tagus, its clustered dwelling-houses dominated by the Cathedral and the Alcazar, the old Imperial City must have looked even then like a relic of Spain's glorious past. Yet it was by no means the provincial, gloomy or decadent place we tend to picture it as being. The Court had been transferred to Madrid in 1567 but this affected Toledo little; it had never been more than the theoretical capital of a nomadic monarchy. A busy industrial center famous for its weavers and armorers, and a crossroads of international traderoutes, Toledo only began to decline after 1609 when the expulsion of the Moors crippled the economic life of the city. A great religious center, it was also an effervescent intellectual center, the home of jurists, poets, scholars and free-thinking humanists. Among them El Greco found both faithful friends and appreciative patrons.

But they had to accept him as he was: capricious and proud, inflexible and contentious where the high price of his pictures was concerned, given to ostentation and extravagance (Jusepe Martínez was shocked to find him hiring musicians to play while he took his meals), but withal a good Christian, a steadfast friend and an "eminent philosopher." There was always a willing circle eager to imbibe the conversation of this eccentric Greek, an inspired talker and a booklover of wide and varied interests. At the Academy founded by the Count of Fuensalida, where the best minds of Toledo sought each other out (Gongora was later one of its most illustrious members), he numbered a host of friends and familiars; very probably he was the unnamed "painter" who figures at the end of the membership roll for that period. But he himself must have entertained

THE BURIAL OF COUNT ORGAZ, 1586.

many a gathering of scholars and intellectuals in the vast suite of rooms he is known to have occupied from 1585 on in the mansion of the Marquis of Villena, a Gothic palace old and dilapidated even in El Greco's time and razed long ago. It stood slightly nearer the river than does the present-day "Casa del Greco," on a superb site, typical of Toledo, in the shadow of the Tránsito synagogue and the Mudejar tower of Santo Tomé, overlooking the gorges of the Tagus.

Taken with the place, El Greco showed no further desire to leave Toledo. For all his dealings with the outside world in the way of commissions and money matters, he delegated full power to Francisco de Preboste, his Italian assistant. His studio was soon producing religious imagery in abundance and its sphere of action reached far beyond the regional confines of New Castile, records proving that at various times, notably in 1597, an intermediary at Seville received pictures intended for export to America. A few dated works enable us to follow the path of his activities. In 1586 he finished his most famous painting, *The Burial of Count Orgaz*. The contract stipulates that the painting shall represent "the procession with the priest and other clerics solemnizing the burial rites of Don Gonzalo"; SS Augustine and Stephen descending from heaven, "one taking him by the feet and the other by the head and lifting him into the tomb"; "a great body of onlookers witnessing the scene and, over the heads of all, the heavens opening out in glory." El Greco complied to the letter with these prescriptions and converted them into a work of art unprecedented in the history of painting: the epitome of a society, the synthesis of heaven and earth, a grand, symphonic dirge ordered with a vigor at once solemn and serene. It marks the zenith of his career and the full maturity of his powers.

◄   THE BAPTISM OF CHRIST, DETAIL, 1596-1600.

Held in balance momentarily, the scales were not long in tipping. The small altarpiece of Talavera la Vieja, rediscovered in 1924 in that outlying village of Estremadura, proves that as early as 1591 El Greco was already elongating forms with a vengeance. Two large-scale works painted in the next few years have now been dispersed. That of the college of Doña María de Aragón in Madrid (dated 1596-1600) undoubtedly included *The Baptism of Christ* (Prado) and very probably *The Annunciation* (Prado, on deposit at the Museo Balaguer at Villanueva y Geltrú) and *The Adoration of the Shepherds* (formerly in the collection of the King of Rumania). The provenance of such kindred works as the *Crucifixion* and *Resurrection* in the Prado is debatable. Of the three altarpieces painted for the Capilla de San José in Toledo in 1597-1599, only that of the main altar *(St Joseph with the Child Jesus* surmounted by a *Coronation of the Virgin)* remains intact; the paintings from the two side altars *(The Virgin with SS Agnes and Thecla* and *St Martin and the Beggar)* now belong to the National Gallery, Washington. All these pictures are distinguished by their high, narrow format; by the vibration of glaucous light on livid colors; by the almost total suppression of space reduced to abstract cloud patterns and vague transpositions of the Toledan landscape lit up beneath crackling thunderstorms; by tall swaying figures, slim, lank and almost weasel-faced, sometimes with an anxious, hungry look in their eyes, sometimes in a disconcerting attitude of fragile grace and relaxation. This is the charm and attraction of El Greco; his painting is a window on an interstellar world beyond the sluggishness of gravity. All these distinctive qualities of his, destined to scandalize the classical-minded 18th century, seem to have been accepted almost as a matter of course by the contemporaries of Santa Teresa and Cervantes.

ST JOSEPH WITH THE CHILD JESUS, C. 1600. ▶

VIEW AND PLAN OF TOLEDO, C. 1605-1610.

SOLITUDE AND EXALTATION

THE years 1603-1604, a turning-point in El Greco's life, brought him to the threshold of old age. Jerónima was presumably dead (no further mention of her being made in the records). There remained Jorge Manuel, his only son and faithful collaborator, though a superficial, irresponsible young man with none of his father's genius; in 1603 he married Alfonsa de los Morales, a handsome but illiterate girl, perhaps to be identified with the young lady in the group portrait in the Pitcairn Collection, in which, presumably, she is surrounded by her only son Gabriel, the old duenna and two servants.

A mysterious relative named Manusos Theotokopoulos, thought to be an elder brother, died late in 1604, gout-stricken and over seventy (the man seems to have drifted to Toledo after being banished from Venice for embezzlement). After 1607 no further mention is made of his devoted assistant Preboste. El Greco himself was soon enfeebled in health; his last contracts always provide for his son's assistance in the work and in 1611, when Pacheco called on him, he was too unwell to show his visitor through his studio. His fame, however, was unimpaired; the municipal authorities of Toledo proclaimed him "one of the most exceptional men in his art, both in this kingdom and abroad," and in 1611 ordered a cenotaph from him for the funeral service of Queen Margaret. Commissions continued to flow in: in 1603 altarpieces for the San Bernardino College of Toledo and the Caridad Hospice of Illescas; in 1607-1608 altarpieces for the Oballe foundation at San Vicente and the San Juan Bautista Hospice. But he was plagued with worry and care; the voluminous file of his lawsuit with the Hospice of Illescas —which, incidentally, reveals many interesting sidelights on El Greco's character and way of life—proves how implacably, for a period of two years, the old artist was persecuted. He was compelled to apply to the Tavera Hospice for an advance on works which ill-health prevented him from completing. He found himself beset by creditors. Returning to the Villena mansion after lodging for several years in another house, he struggled to pay a rent beyond his means for an apartment as immense—it numbered twenty-four rooms—as it was scantily furnished. The inventory of his meager assets, drawn up after his death, makes a touching contrast with that of Velazquez: eight chairs, one bed, one table in black walnut, two coffers, one tablecloth, two bedsheets, seven napkins, his sword, his dagger and a canopy of crimson damask for his bed. The only comforts of his old age were the friendship of Dr Gregorio de

Angulo, a member of the Municipal Council of Toledo, who generously advanced him sizable sums of money several times, and the admiring homage paid him by Fray Hortensio Félix de Paravicino, the preacher and poet.

But the old master, falling back on his most cherished dreams and fancies, outdid himself in his art. Have we perhaps a self-portrait in the famous painting at the Metropolitan Museum of an aged gentleman, his eyelids heavy, his features lined and drawn, but eyes aglow with an inner flame? Perhaps we have him again in the younger man whose presence we note both in *The Martyrdom of St Maurice* and *The Burial of Count Orgaz*, but there is no proof of this. We recognize him unmistakably, however, haughty and outspoken, in such enigmatic quips and aphorisms—reminiscent of Cézanne's in his old age—as were recorded by his contemporaries: "To be dwarfed is the worst thing that can happen to any form," or "A worthy man, Michelangelo, but he never learned how to paint."

His life drew to a close in a magnificent renewal of inspiration. Like Rembrandt and Goya after him, El Greco belonged to that race of artists who, with age, resort increasingly to abridgement, ellipsis, suggestion. His crisp, staccato brushwork, his "impressionistic" handling of form and those "brutal sketches" that so much upset Pacheco vouch for a freedom and unconventionality unmatched in that day. Conforming to the linear rhythms of the ellipse, the pyramid and the spiral, the swirling garments of his figures relieve bodies of all materiality. But at the same time his colors take on the blazing splendor of late autumn—surging harmonies of blues, carmines, ochres and greens. *St Ildefonso* and *The Virgin of Charity* at Illescas and the wonderful *Assumption* at San Vicente in Toledo are his spiritual testament.

Wasted by years of ill health he died on April 7, 1614, leaving many debts unpaid. The only wealth he left behind

PRESUMED SELF-PORTRAIT, C. 1605-1610.

STUDIO WORK: THE FAMILY OF JORGE MANUEL, C. 1605.

consisted of some two hundred canvases, including many small-size replicas of large works and nearly as many drawings, as well as a large library of Greek, Italian and Spanish books; all this is itemized in the two inventories, documents of inestimable importance, brought to light and published by San Román. An imposing funeral ceremony took place at Santo Domingo el Antiguo attended by the monks and religious brotherhoods of Toledo. Although he had expressed the wish to be interred —like Titian in the Frari church of Venice—in the church in which he had painted his first Toledan pictures, and though he had even made a last great *Adoration of the Shepherds* (recently bought by the Prado) intended to stand above his tomb, his wish was respected only for a brief space of time. Jorge Manuel failed to remain on friendly terms with the chapter of Santo Domingo and by 1618 he had broken off relations with them. The body of El Greco was thereupon removed to another convent, San Torcuato, which no longer exists; all trace of his remains has been lost.

But we still possess those "immaterial monuments" raised to his memory by two poets who knew and admired him: the beautiful baroque sonnets of Paravicino and Góngora. And these, like his own fame, are immortal.

EL GRECO'S TOMB

This rugged key, O pilgrim, in the form
Elect and fine of polish'd porphyry
Denies the world the sweetest-flowing brush
That e'er yet quicken'd wood and cloth to life.

Behold his name, whose praise to sound would need
More breath than can through the trumpets of fame
Be blown, on marble slab in letters grave.
Pay it homage and go thy way in life.

Here lies the Greek on whom Nature bestow'd
Her art, Iris the colors of her bow,
To whom Phoebus gave light, not Morpheus shade.

Surely this urn, though adamantine stone,
Drinks in as many tears as it exhales
Perfumes sweet as the barks of Araby.

Luis de Góngora
Sonetos funebres in *Obras en Versos, 1627*

FOR THE TOMB OF A PAINTER
THE GREEK OF TOLEDO

Here lies all that his coffin could immure.
Piety shrouds him and Faith seals the stone
That on him weighs light, for to Heav'n alone
Belongs the part releas'd from earthly cares.

The silent grave cannot deprive the world
Of his fame, and though many an envy war
Against it, never will so bright and high
A star be dimm'd by earthbound vapors' pall.

Apelles' peer, he wrought for better times,
Not vulgar plaudits. His strange art will be
Admir'd in times to come but never match'd.

Crete gave him life and the painter's craft,
Toledo a better homeland where through Death
He kept appointment with Eternity.

Fray Hortensio Felix de Paravicino
Obras póstumas, divinas y humanas, 1641

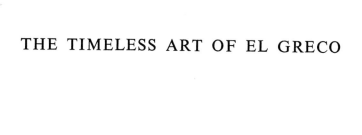

THE TIMELESS ART OF EL GRECO

THE BYZANTINE PAINTER

ERE is an artist of genius who rose to maturity slowly in
three different countries, who was at home in three different languages, in three different cultures whose peculiarities
met and mingled in his subconscious mind. This being so,
El Greco makes a unique object of study in the history of art,
and his career, by its very nature, defies any attempt to divide
it into well-defined periods and zones of influence. In recent
years more and more critics have labored at the task of disen-
tangling the sources behind his art; the lesson of such researches,
seldom conclusive and often contradictory, is that no revelations
can be reasonably hoped for. Nevertheless there remains one
fundamental problem that must be faced: to what extent can
the peculiarities of his art be explained by the dualism of
eastern and western elements? Trained in Italy and transplanted
to Spain, does he prove in the last analysis to be a Byzantine
painter? Or is it more accurate to say that Spain ripened and
shaped his genius? If we are to get even so much as a clear idea
of the problem at hand, it is essential to examine the accepted
facts and isolate as best we can the intermingling undercurrents
that run through his art.

This much can be said at the outset: El Greco, unlike so
many artists who have settled in Spain and married Spanish
women, was never assimilated to his adopted country. We may
even suspect him of a faint but irrepressible yearning for the
far-off island in which he was born. We know anyhow that he
never repudiated his name, language or origins. To the end of
his life—the large capitals of his youthful signature merely
giving way to a fine running hand as he grew old—he signed
his canvases "Domenikos Theotokopoulos" in Greek characters,

MOUNT SINAI (BACK OF THE MODENA POLYPTYCH), BEFORE 1570.

sometimes adding the mention KRES (i.e. Cretan). The Epistle of Paul to Titus, "first bishop of the church of the Cretians," which he puts conspicuously into the hands of St Paul (sacristy, Toledo Cathedral), is proof enough that he looked back fondly on his mother country. Not only did he read Homer, Euripides, Plutarch and other classics in the original Greek, but he had plenty of opportunities to speak the language in Toledo. From 1582 on he acted as an interpreter for the Inquisition and helped quash the charges against a luckless Greek who, after years as a galley-slave in Turkish captivity, had been freed by the Spaniards only to be accused of "Moorish sympathies." By the dawn of the 17th century a small colony of Greeks was thriving in Toledo, some of them transients authorized to collect alms for the ransoming of Christian captives, others permanent residents, such as that other Cretan, Antonio Calosynas, who was a physician and poet of some repute, and also Diogenes Paramonlios and Constantine Phocas, both of whom figure as witnesses in El Greco's will.

So it was only natural that the heritage of his Byzantine past should affect his painting. Though the workings of ancestral memories and blood ties are usually difficult to discern, it is an apparent paradox that they grow ever more perceptible as the years lengthen and cut him off from Greece.

We must be careful about assuming that, as an artist, El Greco received a "Byzantine schooling." As a child, obviously, he had frequent opportunities of seeing frescos and icons in the churches of Candia. But even if local masters taught him the rudiments of the painter's craft, he may well have left his native island out of a desire to break free of an art that had lost all power of renewing itself. By the mid-16th century there were several well-known Cretan painters working in Italy

THE ESPOLIO, 1579. ▶

40

THE HOLY FACE, C. 1600.

(e.g. Michael Damaskinos), in the monasteries of Mount Athos (e.g. Theophanes) and elsewhere—everywhere except in Crete itself. In Venice, with its colony of over four thousand Greeks and the vogue, even in high society, of Byzantine *Madonnas*, this was the heyday of the so-called *Scuola bizantina migliorata* which, while adopting western iconography, retained the traditional eastern technique: tempera painting on a ground very lightly prepared against which finely drawn figures stood out with all the brilliance of enamel or lacquer. These effects linger on in El Greco's early works, such as the *Modena Polyptych*, alongside some rather exotic effects: the strange lunar landscape of Mount Sinai, for example, which recurs in more elaborate form in the small panel owned before the war by Baron Hatvany in Budapest; this panel, no doubt identical with the one that figured in old inventories of the Farnese Palace, is directly inspired by the medieval devotional prints long in vogue with eastern pilgrims.

Then, for a number of years, a veneer of Italianism covered over these primitive undercurrents. But as soon as he reached Toledo El Greco's congenital Byzantinism re-emerged in the Santo Domingo *Resurrection* and the *Espolio*. How account for its resurgence? Was it simply the atmosphere of that Catholic and Moorish city? Was it the large Semitic element of the population, in which Jews and Moors abounded, that awakened echoes and memories of his childhood? Was it the sudden break with Venetian and Roman pomp and the fresh contact with a Christian community whose piety was deep, simple and fervid, and as intimately attached to images of Christ, the Virgin and saints as Cretan piety was to icons? Whatever the causes, his art underwent an orientalizing change as soon as he reached Spain.

First of all we notice what might be diagnosed as Byzantine "outcroppings": iconographical data and compositional patterns which have no precedent in either Spanish or Italian art and which, in varying degrees, approximate to Byzantine prototypes. Among the more striking examples is not only the theme of the *Espolio* (the patiently suffering Christ, the "Elkomenos" so frequent in the 14th-century paintings at Mistra) but even the setting and composition of the theme, which Justi, over half a century ago, likened to those of a mosaic at Monreale in Sicily. The lay-out of El Greco's *Feast in the House of Simon* derives from the same source (i.e. the Byzantine miniature) as *The Last Supper* by his fellow countryman Damaskinos. Even *The Burial of Count Orgaz* betrays compositional elements that are distinctly Byzantine: the lower scene is not without analogy with *The Burial of St Demetrios* at Mistra, while the limp curve of the Count's body in front of the rigid frieze of onlookers, strikes the same immemorial rhythm set by the dead Virgin in front of the apostles in Byzantine *Dormitions*. Even the "Glory" of the upper scene, formed by the Pantocrator with his pointing finger and outstretched arm, the Virgin and St John the Baptist imploring His grace and the double choir of angels and apostles, conforms to the traditional lay-out of the Byzantine Deesis.

Byzantine prototypes are again re-echoed in the Christ of *The Resurrection* at Santo Domingo el Antiguo, a motionless presence in a glowing sky, His arm uplifted graciously, the banner of Faith fluttering behind Him; and again in the angels with enormous wings in *The Baptism of Christ* (Prado).

Many other details might be pointed out in this connection: the Jaws of Hell gulping down the Damned in *The Adoration of the Name of Jesus*; the crystal rocks and the dark trench with the sleeping apostles in *Christ in the Garden of Olives*, which come straight from the Byzantine miniature. Need we invoke the hieratic, inscrutably oriental Savior, His hand lightly lifted in the traditional gesture of blessing, who presides over the

THE FEAST IN THE HOUSE OF SIMON, C. 1605-1610. ▶

Apostolados (i.e. series of apostles) of El Greco? Or, even more suggestive, the strange similarities between his treatment of *The Holy Face* now in the Prado, with Christ's long, loosely falling locks of hair and the haunting gaze of the eyes, and certain Russian icons of the 16th and 17th centuries?

CHRIST IN THE GARDEN OF OLIVES, C. 1600.

But there is something more than this. There is an unmistakable "essence of Byzantium" which, like an underground infiltration, soaks through the whole substructure of his art. Here we are dealing not so much with tangible comparisons as with a prevailing mode of vision. Witness the architecture of faces, with their broad foreheads, arching eyebrows, high cheekbones; the intent and steady gaze of large, round eyes, slightly asymmetrical, which set up a striking parallel between El Greco's portraits of Toledan *hidalgos* and the Fayum portraits of Greco-Egyptian antiquity, halfway between the two being the figures of saints in the Cretan frescos of Mistra. Witness the ever-recurring composition on two planes at once, celestial and terrestrial, divided obliquely one from the other and peopled entirely with surface figures devoid of any recession; this, together with his standing inability to grade scenes hierarchically in space, creates an indubitable spiritual kinship between certain forms of Christian art in the East, notably ivories and miniatures, and such large canvases by El Greco as, for example, *The Martyrdom of St Maurice*. Witness, on a more general level, that hieratic style of unreality which everywhere characterizes El Greco; that serene inadvertence, especially striking in the Christ of the *Espolio* and the main figures of *The Martyrdom of St Maurice*, which screens off his heroes and martyrs from the dramatic action in which they are involved.

His suppression of the third dimension, his indifference to the relative proportions of figures so long as the composition is suitably monumental and rhythmically patterned—this is the law by which the Byzantine mosaic and the Romanesque fresco deriving from it equally abide. Even the inordinate elongation of figures is a latent feature of early mural art. But not the twist and torsion, not the intense sway and vibration El Greco inflicts on them. This is all his own; this marks the limit of his Byzantinism and brings us into another sphere.

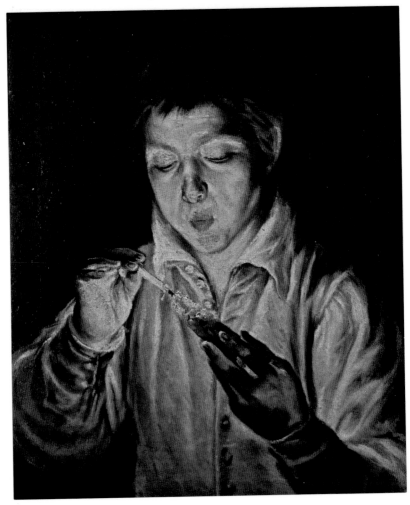

BOY KINDLING A FLAME, C. 1570-1575.

THE ITALIAN PAINTER

E L GRECO set himself to become an Italian painter and became in fact a very good one for as long as he cared to remain in Italy. Thereafter, for the rest of his life, he bore the stamp of a certain Italianism which had become something of a second nature to him, though it had crystallized with other elements and been radically modified.

After the Danish painter Willumsen who, over a quarter of a century ago, published a voluminous, ingenious, but quite uncritical study of El Greco's youthful period, the way was paved for a more sensible and rewarding approach to the subject by such German critics as Mayer, by Anglo-Saxons such as Waterhouse, and above all by such Italians as Venturi, Fiocco and Pallucchini. Much progress was made not only in sorting out his works but in circumscribing the problem of his immediate masters and sources. Here, in addition to his obvious debt to Titian, Tintoretto and Michelangelo, fresh importance was assigned to the presumable influence first of Jacopo Bassano, then of Correggio, Parmigianino and Beccafumi. To re-examine the evidence in detail would lead us beyond the scope of this book. A few points, however, are beyond argument and may be touched on here.

It was thanks to Titian, first of all, that the young Cretan was turned into a "western" painter. Whatever the date of his arrival in Venice, and whether or not he had any personal touch with the old master, then in his eighties, the fact remains that, in that time and place, he could not help seeing countless examples of Titian's best work. From Titian he learned the secret of the portrait, and made the most of it with a talent all his own in the *Portrait of Giulio Clovio*.

Next there was the influence of Jacopo Bassano. Willumsen grossly overstated the case in his fanciful attempt to sift out of the works ascribed to Bassano those that might have been painted by young Greco. Even so, there is no denying the close kinship between Bassano's work and the earliest *Adorations of the Magi* ascribable to El Greco (those in the Benakis Museum, Athens, the Willumsen Collection, Copenhagen, and the Borghese Gallery, Rome), and this not alone by virtue of that elongation of forms noticeably practised by Bassano between 1560 and 1570. An essential facet of that kinship is to be found in Bassano's flair for a popular brand of realism: shepherds, tillers of the soil, rustic night scenes lit up by a glowing candle or a lurid sky. Isarlo has rightly stressed the Europe-wide success of this type of art in the 16th century. A number of genre scenes by El Greco derive from it, most important among them being the *Boy kindling a Flame* in the Naples Pinacoteca.

Next comes the influence of Tintoretto and Michelangelo —a joint influence inasmuch as it must have been through Tintoretto, at Venice, that he first became aware of Michelangelo, who had been dead for six years by the time he reached Rome (in 1570). The very fine drawing rediscovered by Kehrer in the Kupferstichkabinett at Munich, which a centuries-old inscription assigns to El Greco, is a copy of Michelangelo's *Day* in the Medici Chapel in Florence, but it was made from a replica known to have been in Venice in 1563. Then there is the *Martyrdom of St Sebastian* in Palencia Cathedral, a key work of the very first years in Spain which has not been given the attention it deserves; this seems to be an anticipated transposition of Tintoretto's *St Sebastian* at the Scuola di San Rocco, which dates from 1576 (after El Greco had left Venice) but which he must have seen in an unfinished state or in the preparatory sketches; both works, anyhow, derive directly from Michelangelo's *Haman* in the Sistine Chapel. The difference is that El Greco's martyr is not a stormy hero overcome and crushed, but an uncomplaining ascetic resigned to his fate.

PORTRAIT OF GIULIO CLOVIO, C. 1570.

The fundamental incompatibility of two great temperaments, one dramatic, the other contemplative, naturally set limits on the influence Tintoretto could bring to bear on El Greco; that influence, nevertheless, is so well marked that we are entitled to wonder if El Greco may not have been working in his studio round about 1564 when the master first began the immense cycle of works for the Scuola di San Rocco. Take for example the unconventional width of the composition, the perspective vista of stairs and colonnades, the porticos in the background opening on the sky, the swelling plenitude of forms, the details of children, bird-cages, rabbits and dogs, which we find in the early version of *Christ driving the Traders from the Temple* (Cook Collection, Richmond, Surrey) and *The Healing of the Blind Man* (Dresden and Parma); take the tall, flashing figure of Christ

THE HEALING OF THE BLIND MAN, C. 1570.

CHRIST DRIVING THE TRADERS FROM THE TEMPLE, C. 1570-1575.

in the second version of *Christ driving the Traders from the Temple* (Minneapolis), with its livid gleams of greenish light. After this it would be foolish to deny the influence of Tintoretto.

The very least that can be said—and this is a great deal— is that both men worked in much the same way, making figure sketches from small statues modeled in clay or wax. By setting these beside a lamp or a torch they could study the flickering play of light on forms. When Pacheco visited El Greco he was amazed to find a whole roomful of such statuettes.

As for Michelangelo, his tremendous shadow hung over El Greco throughout his stay in Rome and, perhaps by his spirited reaction against it, helped him to find himself. It is surely not by chance that in the lower righthand corner of the Minneapolis version of *Christ driving the Traders from the Temple* we find, beside that of Titian, a portrait of Michelangelo (a third figure is easily identified as Giulio Clovio, while a fourth may represent either Raphael or El Greco himself). If his indifference to color nettled El Greco, it is also true that the plastic force of his figures preyed on his mind even after he had migrated to Spain.

If the small *Last Judgment* which came to light a few years ago in a Rhenish collection should prove to be by El Greco (that proof is still forthcoming), this strange sketch, with its reminiscences of Michelangelo couched in a wholly medieval conception of perspective, would go far towards explaining El Greco's boast that, any time he chose, he could make of the *Last Judgment* in the Sistine Chapel a work genuinely devout and seemly. One authenticated picture, the small *Pietà* in Philadelphia, is indeed patterned after Michelangelo's *Entombment* in the National Gallery, London. But the figures, almost anaemic in comparison, are considerably scaled down.

The reason is that by the time El Greco had reached Rome the vogue of Michelangelo had already been superseded by that of the younger Tuscan and Roman mannerists, such men as Pontormo, Salviati, Taddeo Zuccaro. Their stock-in-trade was tall, willowy figures with well-cambered bodies, a springy step and S-shaped folds in their garments; in their canvases we have the angels and warriors of El Greco's *Martyrdom of St Maurice* (together with his clear, cold colors) in embryonic form. In the

THE MARTYRDOM OF ST SEBASTIAN, C. 1580.

work of the Sienese "luminist" Domenico Beccafumi we find not only the prototypes of El Greco's angels but the same gamut of mysterious whites.

By the time he left for Spain he was saturated with the forms and images referred to above. He poured them out, eclectically and prudently, in the Santo Domingo paintings. *The Assumption* is a direct descendant of that by Titian in the church of the Frari in Venice, but a hint of mannerism is also perceptible in certain gestures of the apostles. *The Adoration of the Shepherds* is a nightpiece recalling Bassano in every way—though mingling with it is a dim recollection of Correggio's *Night*, a small copy of which (Contini-Bonacossi Collection) is ascribed to El Greco. The colossal figures of the two SS John are refined restatements of Michelangelo. The composition of *The Trinity* (Prado) is patterned after a print by Dürer; Michelangelo reappears in the sculptural solidity of the divine group, and mannerism in the crystal-clear, crystal-hard color-scheme, while the angels recall those supporting the dead Christ in a painting by Taddeo Zuccaro in the Borghese Gallery, Rome.

Mannerist elements continued to gain ground in his work. As he was immersed in the atmosphere of Toledo, his memories of Venice faded, and a cool range of blues, carmines and greys ousted the shadowed golds and ambers of Italian days. Purely anecdotal figures became a thing of the past; lay-outs were tightened up and simplified to the point of starkness (the fine *Descent from the Cross* in the Niarchos Collection shows what happened in Spain to a composition no doubt inspired by Tintoretto). All that remained intact was his fondness for architectural settings, as seen in the background of the many *Feasts in the House of Simon*. As against this, his work was soon impregnated with mannerism—not only with its outward show but with its stock compositional patterns: intersecting curves forming elongated ovals and, in the foreground, framing figures shown half-length or seen from behind. Suffice it to mention works as varied as *The Coronation of the Virgin* (Talavera), *The Immaculate Conception* (Toledo), *The Pentecost* (Prado).

Perhaps the attraction which the Escorial held for him—anyhow for a few years' time—served to stimulate this trend, for it was the stronghold of mannerism in Spain. On the other hand, he could have had no very high opinion of anything he saw there and it is safe to say that, if his painting took the direction just described, it was wholly in obedience to the artist's innermost aspirations. His own mannerism, furthermore, never lapsed into the academic formulas that handicapped the Italians at every turn. The reason is that his serpentine figures, dramatized by great bursts of light, always seem to be uncoiling themselves in restless excitement, thus exteriorizing an inner conflict of which he was unaware in Italy but which may have dawned on him with the failure of *St Maurice*: the ineluctable feud between the Byzantine unreality in which his own art was steeped and the dramatic dynamism of space cultivated by the Italian Renaissance, by Michelangelo and Tintoretto.

We only get into trouble if, in this connection, we fall back on labels whose meaning is too vast and hazy. If we accept "baroque" and "classical" as mere categories of the mind and proceed, as Eugenio d'Ors suggested, to set up "the world of fluttering forms" against "the world of leaning forms," then we are entitled to oppose El Greco to Poussin as archetypes, respectively, of the baroque and the classical. But if we associate "baroque" with amplitude of form, billowing drapery and effects of illusionist perspective, then we had better be careful about calling El Greco a "baroque" painter. Rather, as Kehrer described him, he is "the last of the mannerists." What is more, he proved to be the only mannerist capable of putting exhaustive investigation of form to the service of new expressive values. And it was Spain that opened his eyes to these values.

THE SPANISH PAINTER

Crete gave him life and the painter's craft,
Toledo a better homeland...

THESE lines of Paravicino express an undeniable truth. It is hard to imagine what would have become of El Greco had he remained in Italy, where so many centuries of tradition acting on his restless, receptive spirit might in the end have checked the upswing of his own originality. He would then have had his place among the second-rank Italian masters, that legion of notable mediocrities. As it is, he was nearing forty when, all of a sudden, after a few years in Spain, his genius burst to the surface.

Did Toledo have anything more for him than the negative shock-value of an abrupt uprooting, a sharp break with his own past? Or did it plant him firmly in the midst of a living tradition that nourished the deepest aspirations of his soul?

What can he be said to owe to Toledo? And what did he give her in return? To what extent does he have his place cut out for him in the history of Spanish painting, as, for example, Lully has his in the history of French music? Most students of El Greco devote less attention to this question than to elucidating the Byzantine and Italian sources of his style—perhaps because they take his place in Spanish art for granted. Between the thoroughgoing "annexationism" of Cossío—for whom El Greco is the spiritual father of Velazquez, the very incarnation of the Spanish genius, whose austerity, whose grave and mournful mysticism he expressed with increasingly pungent realism—and the reaction to the opposite extreme of Mayer—who sees in El Greco the "oriental artist" landed by a quirk of fate in Toledo, where he sank no roots and left no posterity

◄   ST MARTIN AND THE BEGGAR, C. 1600-1605.

59

—there is room for distinctions and finer shades of analysis, and these time will bring out and certify. For the moment, in the history of Spanish painting and iconography in its Golden Age, many chapters are still so incomplete that no proper conclusions can be drawn.

One point, however, brooks no discussion. Toledo provided El Greco with a mine of new material particularly stimulating for an artist fresh from the great cities of Renaissance Italy: an aristocratic, homogeneous, god-fearing, militaristic society whose way of life complied with rigid standards. There was of course another Toledo, easy-going and picaresque, which Cervantes wrote about in his *Novelas ejemplares* and which El Greco's *hidalgos* tend to make us forget. But the circles in which El Greco moved were those that set the tone of the most intensely Catholic city of Spain, very different from the mercantile, cosmopolitan atmosphere of Seville. This closed circle of priests, jurists and retired military men must have struck a foreign artist looking upon it for the first time as a kind of free stage whose actors offered the eye endless and remarkable combinations of light and form: dress uniformly dark, with the dazzling white of pleated ruffs, short-cropped hair and elegantly tapered goatees—human architecture reduced to its essentials, with nothing about it to deflect an eye intent on penetrating to the soul.

The models he found in Toledo were so much to his liking that he worked them into his religious paintings. We find the same young aristocrat, proud, courteous and melancholic, shown first as St Maurice, later as St Martin, while the centurion of the *Espolio* is a beribboned Spanish army captain, a veteran of the Duke of Alba's Flemish and Italian campaigns. He portrayed these people exactly as he must have seen them in daily life.

THE MARTYRDOM OF ST MAURICE, C. 1580-1582. ▶

Gr. 24

LEFT: PRESUMED SELF-PORTRAIT,
DETAIL FROM THE BURIAL OF COUNT ORGAZ, 1586.

ST MAURICE, DETAIL FROM THE MARTYRDOM OF ST MAURICE, C. 1580-1582. ▶

62

The Burial of Count Orgaz, for example, is an incomparable gallery of portraits, "realistically painted" and including "many illustrious men of our time" (wrote the historian of Toledo Francisco de Pisa). On the right, the officiating clergy, surpliced for the occasion; on the left, the Franciscan friars, perhaps from the neighboring convent of San Juan de los Reyes, and the torch-bearing choirboy (a portrait of Jorge Manuel at the age of eight). Of the twenty-odd gentlemen in the background only one is identifiable: Antonio Covarrubias, of whom El Greco made several portraits. The others are skillfully differentiated from one another by age, the cut of the face and the turn of the head. No one betrays any sorrow or surprise; all is dignified composure and attentiveness. A single masterpiece of modern painting imparts the same sense of re-entering a defunct world, of sharing in the life of a small human community, and that is Courbet's *Funeral at Ornans* (Louvre). The parallel is often drawn between the two pictures, and rightly so. From the strictly spiritual point of view, however, Courbet is insignificant beside El Greco.

There are still more of these ascetic, contemplative Spaniards in the lower part of other religious pictures: the Dean of the Chapter Don Diego de Castilla, in *The Resurrection* in Santo Domingo el Antiguo; the anonymous cleric and layman at the foot of *Christ on the Cross* in the Louvre; the priest of Santo Tomé, Don Andrés Núñez de Madrid, standing before a *Christ on the Cross* in the small church of Martín Muñoz de las Posadas (province of Segovia). And in his final masterpiece at the Hospice of Illescas we find a whole company of unknown *hidalgos* sheltered by the *Virgin of Charity*, in keeping with the medieval tradition of the "Virgin of Mercy," beneath the broad folds of her immense, lightly floating mantle.

DETAIL OF THE BURIAL OF COUNT ORGAZ, 1586. ▶

Elsewhere, El Greco's portraits of Toledan contemporaries make up the bulk of his non-religious work. The Prado possesses a superb set of these: some ten canvases largely got together by Velazquez for the collection of Philip IV; they represent one quarter of the signed or accepted portraits by El Greco now scattered throughout the world. A few portraits of women exist, but only one is signed: the *Portrait of a Woman with a Flower in her Hair* in the Stirling-Maxwell Collection.

Among the male portraits, it is notable that the great of this world are few in number and the greatest of these are three cardinals. The earliest in history, Cardinal Tavera, was painted last; humanist and church builder, founder of the Hospice of San Juan Bautista, he died in 1545. This portrait, like Alonso Berruguete's sculpture for the tomb, must have been made from a death-mask; this ivory face above a brilliant carmine-violet cape is one of the most moving works of El Greco's last period. *The Portrait of Cardinal Quiroga*, on the other hand, is still Italianate and may therefore be dated to about 1580. Between them stands one of the supreme masterpieces of painting: *The Portrait of Cardinal Don Fernando Niño de Guevara*, archbishop of Seville in 1596 and grand inquisitor. In the latter capacity he visited Toledo in 1600; El Greco must have painted his portrait at the time. Standing above and beyond all others is the amazing vision of this elderly churchman seated amidst the robes of his office, a squat, pyramidal figure with a shrewd pair of eyes gazing slightly to one side from behind thick glasses. This picture is exceptional among the portraits El Greco made at Toledo both for its cherry-red color-scheme (from which Velazquez wisely took a lesson a half-century later in his *Portrait of Pope Innocent X*) and for the fact that it is a full-length figure in a well-delineated setting.

PORTRAIT OF CARDINAL DON FERNANDO NIÑO DE GUEVARA, C. 1600. ▶

66

DETAIL OF THE PORTRAIT OF CARDINAL DON FERNANDO NIÑO DE GUEVARA.

DETAIL OF THE PORTRAIT OF CARDINAL DON FERNANDO NIÑO DE GUEVARA.

Of the lay portraits only one is that of a great nobleman whom we can positively identify: the Duke of Benavente (Musée Bonnat, Bayonne). The others are of functionaries and officials (Rodrigo Vázquez, chairman of the Board of Finance of Castile), jurists and humanists (Dr Rodrigo de la Fuente, physician and poet; Antonio Covarrubias, an eminent doctor of canon law and a Greek scholar who presented his friend El Greco with his translation of Xenophon and of whom two other portraits exist; his elder brother Diego Covarrubias, bishop of Segovia; Jerónimo de Cevallos, a jurist with a fondness for letters); then there are monks and friars of various orders, most notable of whom is the Trinitarian Fray Hortensio Félix de Paravicino (two of his portraits are masterpieces: the small portrait in the Casa Torres Collection, Madrid, and the large seated figure, relaxed and pensive, in the Boston Museum of Fine Arts); the poet crowned with a laurel wreath in The Hermitage, Leningrad (Alonso de Ercilla y Zúñiga?); a sculptor chipping at a bust of Philip II (Pompeo Leoni?); the unknown painter with palette and poised brush in Seville Museum; and, lastly, the many portraits of unknown *hidalgos*.

Anonymity being the general rule, the problem of dating becomes twice as difficult. The more "calligraphic" portraits (that of Rodrigo Vázquez, for instance, in the Prado) may be assigned to the early years in Toledo. The portraits of Cevallos and Paravicino, even if the age of the model did not prove them to be late works, would strike us at once by the terseness and roughcast of the brushwork. On the other hand, the more or less pronounced elongation of faces is definitely not a reliable criterion for the dating of portraits; better, as Camón Aznar suggests, is the criterion of "anguish."

What are we to understand by this? The essential feature of all El Greco's portraits, whether busts or heads, is intensity of expression. The beauty and freedom of the technique he had

PORTRAIT OF DON JERÓNIMO DE CEVALLOS, C. 1605-1610.

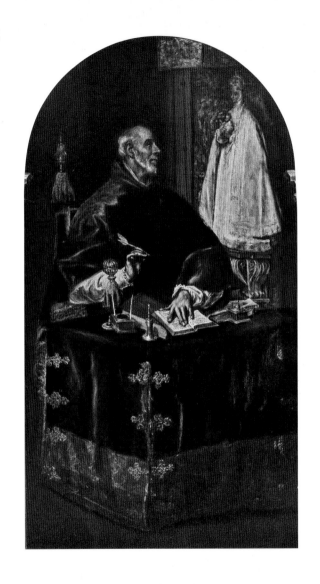

72

learned in Venice, together with subtle gradations of values in the gamut of blacks and whites, gave life to his restricted palette. He had no need of ornaments or accessories to enliven his portraits; once he included a sword-hilt, once or twice a book, but this was exceptional. He improved on the traditional severity of the Spanish court portrait, whose pattern, set once and for all in the mid-16th century by Sanchez Coello, was to hold good until the coming of the Bourbons to the Spanish throne (1700). El Greco apparently could not help coming under the sway of that mania for three-quarter poses, static and inflexible, which infected most painters of that day. But against his neutral background two elements became extraordinarily alive: eyes and hands. "Winged hands," wrote Unamuno, who glorified El Greco as "one of the few artists to show us that hands reveal far more than words do." At the same time faces tell of anxiety, of a resigned yet virile melancholy, as in the portrait of an aged gentleman in the Prado (no. 806 in the catalogue). Looking at the portraits, we might almost imagine an evolution in the opposite direction to that of the religious figures, an evolution in which the type takes increasing precedence over the individual; in this case the last portraits would be those weighted with lassitude and perceptibly conveying the hint of a well-kept secret. An any rate, the Toledo cycle of portraits stands alone and apart in the whole of European painting. They have no more in common with the stiff, cold, lifeless faces of Sanchez Coello and Pantoja de la Cruz than with the lively French portraits of the Court of the Valois.

Aside from the living models she gave him, did Toledo have anything to teach El Greco in the way of technique, craftsmanship or style? So stated, the question is readily answered. What, indeed, could so proficient a painter, scholar and geometer into

◀ ST ILDEFONSO WRITING AT THE VIRGIN'S DICTATION, C. 1605.

DETAIL OF ST ILDEFONSO WRITING AT THE VIRGIN'S DICTATION.

the bargain, justly proud of the lessons learnt at first hand in Venice and Rome, what could he think of those plodding provincials—Correa and Comontes, for example—who so dutifully carried on the Gothic tradition of ingenuous naturalism while pressing all the vigor out of it? Surely he smiled at what he found in Toledo, which by that time had lagged far behind Madrid and the Escorial and had ceased to be affected by the invigorating international trends that had gathered such force

DETAIL OF ST ILDEFONSO WRITING AT THE VIRGIN'S DICTATION.

in Spain (represented, early in the 16th century, by such men as Francisco de Amberes and Juan de Borgoña). The truth is that the Renaissance was anything but a blessing to Spanish painting, which, from a living force at the beginning of the 16th century, had dwindled to paralysis by the end of the century. A single great name might have attracted El Greco's attention, but it was that of a sculptor, a follower of Michelangelo: Alonso Berruguete. More than one attempt has been made to detect the possible influence of his work (he died in 1561) on the evolution of El Greco, but nothing conclusive or even convincing has come of them. The distortions and expressive wrenching of his figures are hardly less than those of El Greco's. But Italian sources common to the two artists more than suffice to explain the similarities between them.

No Spanish artist can be credited with influencing El Greco, but what did influence him to some extent was the tenor and tradition of Spanish art as a whole, the type of commissions he received and the type of picture he was expected to produce, and the fixed laws to which Spanish altarpieces conformed—the reredos enjoying in Spain, be it remembered, the same universal favor enjoyed by the fresco in Italy. Altarpieces consisting of many parts, lavishly embellished with sculpture and painting, made up largely of tall narrow panels suitable for fitting into intercolumniation, apparently answered to the natural bias of El Greco's artistic temperament. And commissions based on these data gave him frequent opportunities to paint "processional" figures, imposing and solemn, now gorgeous, now ascetic, which stand out against landscapes or backgrounds altogether bare. Such images as these abound in the work of the Spanish Primitives, and the clever craftsmen of the Escorial had not repudiated them; they had even "improved" on them

PORTRAIT OF FRAY HORTENSIO FELIX DE PARAVICINO, C. 1610. ►

by disposing the apostles and martyrs two by two on the altar-pieces staggered at intervals throughout the basilica. The whole team of Spanish artists employed by Philip II—Luis de Carvajal, Sanchez Coello, and many others—was turned on to this task; and Navarrete, the mute painter who died young at Toledo in 1579, had contributed some of the finest of these figures. He was an artist whom El Greco might well have respected; Navarrete was a Venetian at heart, having learnt his art, if not in Italy, then from the splendid Titians in the king's collections.

Now El Greco, whether out of spontaneous sympathy with them or in a deliberate effort to comply with the tastes of Toledo, followed the lead of these men. Several times, in small-size works, he painted pairs of saints, either in an interior (*SS Peter and Paul* at Barcelona Museum) or against a lowlying background of russet hills vaguely resembling the Toledo countryside (the two *SS John* at San Juan Bautista in Toledo, *St John the Evangelist and St Francis* and *St Andrew and St Francis* at the Prado). More numerous are the solitary figures whose utter simplicity achieves an epic grandeur; some lean on a staff, others on their cross, in a rockbound landscape sometimes fringed with the towered silhouette of Toledo; such are *St James the Greater* (former Herzog Collection, Budapest), *St Andrew* (Zuloaga Museum, Zumaya), *St Joseph with the Child Jesus* (Capilla de San José, Toledo). The latter is remarkable for the youthful, virile figure of the protecting saint who exactly reflects an iconographical creation peculiar to Santa Teresa. The chapel the painting decorates stands, as a matter of fact, on the very site of the house in which Santa Teresa lived, and it was, moreover, the first sanctuary in Christendom to be dedicated to St Joseph.

Another figure of the same type, even taller and slenderer, is that of *St Bernardin of Siena* (El Greco Museum, Toledo). Holding a staff surmounted by the Sacred Monogram of Christ (which he is said to have invented), he is the very symbol of detachment, standing forlorn against a livid sky, with three bishop's mitres on the ground beside him; these represent the three bishoprics this famous preacher-saint refused.

Commissioned to paint bishops and deacons in their heavy dalmatics, gorgeous with interwoven gold and floral patterns alternating with exquisite embroideries, El Greco produced some of his masterpieces: not only St Augustine and St Stephen in *The Burial of Count Orgaz*, but the *St Lawrence* in the college of Monforte and above all the *Archbishop of Toledo* (St Eugene or St Ildefonso?) which once decorated the high altar at San Vicente in Toledo and which Velazquez purchased for the Escorial together with its pendant, the grandiose *St Peter*, his robes billowing out in a storm wind. At the same time he made several portraits in miniature: the pair of gentlemen, signed, formerly in the Sobejano Collection, Valladolid, and *The Portrait of Dr Pisa* in the collection of Dr Marañon, Madrid. Byzantine traditions coupled with the lessons of Clovio no doubt prompted him to try his hand at the miniature. Then, too, the large school of miniaturists working at the Escorial set him an example he may have followed to some extent.

But he too set the Spaniards an example, for it was he who formulated and popularized—perhaps even invented—those cycles of *Apostolados* which were destined to become one of the type forms of Spanish religious painting.

By the 17th century these sets of twelve apostles, formed by separate pictures, shown either half-length or full-length, and often presided over by a thirteenth picture of the Savior, were an indispensable decorative element in the naves of Spanish churches. In addition to innumerable lesser artists, this theme inspired such masters as Ribera and Zurbaran. But none of theirs match the suggestive power of El Greco's *Apostolados*, whose popularity is proved by the many variant sets he was called upon to make. At least twelve such cycles, either by the master or his studio, can still be traced, though nearly all are now dispersed; there must have been many more, judging by the number of isolated apostles that have found their way into museums and private collections. Only three sets are complete: those in Toledo Cathedral, in the El Greco Museum, Toledo, and in the collection of the Marquis of San Félix at Oviedo. Eight pictures of a fourth set from Almadrones (Guadalajara) entered the Prado after the Civil War of 1936-1939.

All appear to date from the last twenty years of El Greco's career. Their composition—which usually included St Paul—was more or less standardized. The most curious variant is that in Toledo Cathedral where St Bartholomew is replaced by St Luke, the painter of the Virgin; he holds an open Book of Hours with a miniature of the Virgin and Child well in view.

Christ alone in these cycles, His hand lifted in blessing, radiates warmth and gentleness. But the ardor of His goodness and grandeur burns in the eyes of His disciples and sets their being—particularly their hands—aquiver. Alongside massive greybeards (St Andrew, St Philip, St Matthew) and a strangely ascetic St Paul or a romantically melancholy St John, some of the younger saints, gaunt and haggard, with scraggly beards, cut the figure of hallucinated anchorites (St Thomas in the El Greco Museum, and especially St Bartholomew, his robes as white as snow, holding a small grinning demon at the end of a chain).

We must look to another set of works, however, to find the real pledge of El Greco's deep affinity with the Spanish soul. These are the devotional pictures, meant to induce compunction, penitence and prayer—those images which play so large a part in the spiritual exercises laid down by St Ignatius, Santa Teresa and the Blessed Juan de Avila.

After his initial success at Toledo, El Greco was besieged with orders for work in local country churches, in modest

ST BARTHOLOMEW, C. 1605-1610.

convents endowed by devout gentlefolk, in the oratories of private estates. We have sufficient proof of this in all the pictures brought to light since, in the past half-century or so, El Greco has been the object of active investigations, and not alone in the immediate vicinity of Toledo but in the whole of New Castile—and not alone autograph and studio works but any number of belated copies, often very uncouth, which nevertheless testify to the fidelity with which the originals, having imposed themselves, were thereafter followed.

The motive power and conviction behind El Greco's highly refined mannerism sprang directly from a keen and vigorous sensibility. The same has rightly been said of a slightly older contemporary of his, a provincial painter working further west, in Estremadura: Luis de Morales, whose art had also met with King Philip's disapproval, whose studio at Badajoz, however, had become a regional art center of considerable influence. Morales grafted mannerist recipes on to traditional Gothic forms much as El Greco grafted them on to hieratic Byzantine forms. The difference is that the latter's grasp and handling of them goes farther, immeasurably farther, in subtlety, craftsmanship and visionary power than does Morales' smooth, painstaking technique. We need only compare the range of subject-matter embraced by each to get an idea of El Greco's vast superiority. Morales seldom ventured away from three themes: the Virgin suckling her Child, Christ attached to the pillar, the Pietà. El Greco dealt with every variety of evangelical and hagiographical subject, not to mention the replicas he made of such large-scale compositions as the *Espolio*. We have the Virgin as an adolescent (Prado, Strasbourg), a candid Castilian girl looking upon the world with wide-eyed wonder. We have the series of *Holy Families* (the Virgin suckling or gazing at the Child, usually flanked by St Anne and St Joseph), whose atmosphere of anxious tenderness is precisely that of the

DETAIL OF THE NATIVITY, C. 1605.

ST DOMINIC KNEELING BEFORE THE CRUCIFIX, C. 1595-1600.

Romance of Our Lady with the Child Jesus in her Arms of José de
Valdivieso. The slightly mannered, often poignant verses of
this Toledan poet, a contemporary of El Greco, are almost like
a written commentary to his paintings. This atmosphere also
pervades one of El Greco's rarest and tenderest creations, the
Farewell of Jesus to Mary as He takes leave of His mother and
enters on His earthly mission (Camón Aznar holds the picture
to be a meeting after the Resurrection, but this interpretation
is less convincing). The pent-up eloquence of the scene is all
in its tender grace and melancholy; only the meeting of hands
and the shy gaze into each other's eyes express the sweet sorrow
of parting.

To those who meditate upon the Passion El Greco offers an
unforgettable image: Christ bearing the Cross and crowned
with thorns, His eyes moist with tears, the angular lines of
forms re-echoing those of Flamboyant Gothic. More remote,
more elegiac than tragic, but no less moving, are the *Crucifixions*
of various sizes and formats, but seldom life-size, like those in
the Louvre and Prado. The smaller ones, intensely devotional
works, must have been intended for oratories; such are those
in the Cincinnati Art Museum and in the San Vicente Museum,
Toledo. A tall cross, bearing the gently curving body of Christ,
spans the picture vertically against a twilight background;
Jerusalem is obviously Toledo and on the Alcantara Bridge
rides a tiny Roman horseman.

The series of "penitents" includes many versions of the
Tears of St Peter (Cathedral and El Greco Museum, Toledo);
many *Magdalens*, whose opulent figure in the earlier versions was
always Venetian, while no less lovely are the increasingly ascetic
Magdalens of the last period (Worcester Museum, Massachusetts,
and Paradas Collection, Seville); several versions of *St Jerome*
in his desert retreat beside an inscrutable death's head. Greater
importance must be attached to the pictures of *St Francis*,

however, a theme to which El Greco reverted again and again, almost obsessively. The theme of *St Dominic kneeling before the Crucifix* undoubtedly inspired several of his most moving devotional paintings, subtly dramatized by the contrast between the white robe and the black tippet and mantle (Cathedral and San Vicente Museum, Toledo). But when we remember that Camón Aznar records over one hundred and twenty pictures of St Francis—running from large altar paintings to small devotional images, from autograph works to studio replicas—then we realize that this is one of the keynotes in El Greco's entire output. Childhood memories may partly account for this fact, St Francis (together with the Virgin) being one of the most popular objects of devotion in the island of Crete, where his worship was a powerful factor of reconciliation between Orthodox and Catholics. El Greco had a way of picturing the Italian saint that appealed as intensely to scholars and theologians as it did to the army of the faithful. Pacheco, usually so reticent, had to admit that none could match him: "Certain it is that if Antonio Mohedano had followed these instructions (those set down in the *Chronicle of the Minorite Friars*), he would have been in my estimation the best painter of this saint known to our age. But we are obliged to bestow this honor on Dominico Greco, inasmuch as he more suitably complied with the facts of history."

What El Greco complied with was not so much the "facts of history" as the orthodox iconographical data relating to his subject. For the essential characteristic of his St Francis is that of being lifted completely from his historical context. Nothing is left of his native Umbria, of the proverbial kindness of the Poverello, of his miracles or his love of men and beasts. The only historical episode alluded to is the stigmatization.

ST BERNARDIN OF SIENA, 1603. ▶

The very early versions (for example the small panel in the Zuloaga Musem) are unusual in that they surround St Francis and Brother Leo with a wooded landscape. Before long the setting was stripped down to a barren, rockbound, near-abstract decor, and St Francis was turned into a haggard, cadaverous ascetic (for whom the gaunt Franciscan in *The Burial of Count Orgaz* may well have been the model). Recurring types and attitudes, however, divide all these pictures into some eight or ten sets which seem to have developed in parallel fashion rather than successively. They may be said to fall under the following headings: St Francis receiving the stigmata, with arms outspread like a great wounded bird, shown either half-length alone or kneeling in front of Brother Leo (Cerralbo Museum, Madrid); St Francis at prayer, bowing gently down before a crucifix or gazing blissfully heavenward (Lille Museum). Perhaps the most compelling and original series is that which Cossío so aptly baptized the "Hamlet St Francis" (Colegio de Doncellas Nobles, Toledo, and Valdés Collection, Bilbao): the saint on bended knee, with downcast eyes, his short black beard framed in a tight-fitting cowl, meditating on a skull held in his two hands. These images, especially the last, fixed the standard Spanish type of St Francis for a long time to come. Plagiarized copies are to be found up to the end of the 17th century (e.g. the St Francis signed and dated 1696 by Blas Muñoz of Murcia, now in the El Greco Museum). Variants are to be found in the different paintings of St Francis by Zurbaran and in the sculptures of him by Pedro de Mena. No other creation by El Greco had so marked and profound an effect on the Spanish sensibility.

Is it to be inferred from this that El Greco developed into a truly Spanish painter, an authentic *castizo*? The answer is no. There is a wide gulf indeed between the native Spanish feeling for the concrete and matter-of-fact and El Greco's irrepressible soarings into poetic unreality. And this is even true—perhaps

ST FRANCIS RECEIVING THE STIGMATA, C. 1600-1605.

truest of all—when his art deals with the supernatural. God descends to earth and man there awaits His miracle-working intervention—such is the tradition of Spanish painting. Not so with El Greco; in his painting man wrenches free of earthly ties to attain to union with God, or else a glorious host of the Elect serve to conjoin heaven and earth. Ever since the Middle Ages Spanish painting has teemed with mystical dialogues; but these always take place before the altar (as in Pedro Berruguete's *Christ and St Peter Martyr*) or in the monkish intimacy of convent cells or cloisters (as in Zurbaran's *Christ appearing to Father Salmeron*). Such "everyday" visits of divinity are the just reward of a saintly life and received with a joyful heart but with no particular surprise.

This fraternity between heaven and earth is by no means alien to El Greco's art. The presence of the two saints, heavenly visitants amidst the assembled clerics and nobles, gives the fullness of its spiritual and formal harmony to *The Burial of Count Orgaz* and makes it certainly the most Spanish of all 16th-century Spanish paintings. Other instances of divine intervention in earthly matters might be cited: the heaven-sent knight (St Louis?) commending the kneeling Knight of St James in a great white cape (who is, according to a later inscription of dubious authenticity, Captain Julian Romero, "El de las Azanas"); or even St Ildefonso of Illescas ecstatically writing at the Virgin's dictation, the splendid and unsurpassed prototype of many a 17th-century ascetic and doctor of the church seen in the familiar surroundings of the cell.

But the presentation of the last-named picture—the strangely tense and oscillating angle of vision poised on the three receding edges of the table and the receding line of the cheekbone—is rooted in a spirit that is anything but the spirit of Spanish art. Possibly—as ingeniously suggested by Dr Marañon in a recent study—the Spanish genius, being half Semitic, half Celtiberian, takes dual and even contradictory forms at certain periods of history. Perhaps the idealistic piety of El Greco, intellectual and easterner that he was, felt more at home with the mystical mind of the 16th century than with the naturalism and ardent popular faith that set in, like a tide of reaction, in the following century. It is all too obvious that as soon as he was dead his disciples and imitators, Tristan and Orrente among others, blew up his lean forms, weighted them down with earthiness, and pressed his well-equated "tenebrist luminism" into the service of the realism and sculptural effects then coming into fashion. Even for the 16th century there is no justification for the assumption that El Greco's visions are a pictorial transcription of those of contemporary Spanish mystics, whose trances and emotions they purport to interpret or express. All the parallels so far drawn between passages in the writings of Santa Teresa and El Greco's *Resurrection* and *Pentecost* are not only unconvincing, they are extremely far-fetched. The same is true of the poetic imagery of St John of the Cross; by no stretch of the imagination do his flowered fields, gushing springs and pastoral hills have any counterpart in El Greco's flashing abstractions.

That El Greco was an ardent believer is beyond question, and after the salvo of enthusiasm with which the age of Philip II renewed the ardor of Spanish catholicism, even his most disconcerting paintings were respectfully acknowledged by the very men in authority who least understood them. But the language of painters is not that of mystics, and the problems conditioning the painter's language lie too far afield, anyhow in this instance, to justify the parallel. Besides, the problems that haunted El Greco fall into a distinctly liberal order of meditation—that of a man of the Renaissance—embracing poetry, science and the purely technical side of the painter's art. His canvases are a system or an image of the world, elaborated throughout a lifetime and brought to perfection in the creations of his old age.

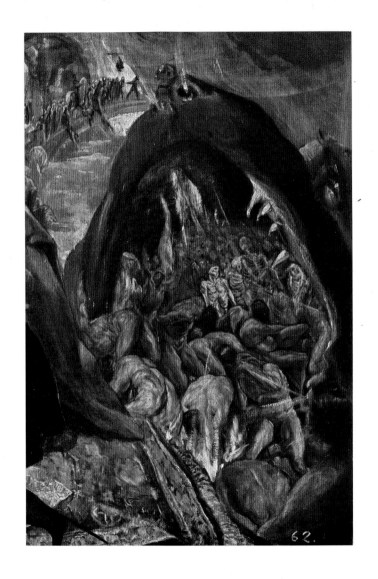

62.

THE VISIONARY

IF WE call those artists visionaries who, after a given time, are less attracted to what they see around them than to the visions of their mind's eye, and who engross themselves in an attempt to record the dreams and nightmares that stir within them, then El Greco was not a visionary till late in life. That he was destined to become one, however, was obvious from the start. In the *Modena Polyptych*, not only does the Mount Sinai panel already answer to a fantastic or anyhow "surreal" conception of landscape, but the central panel is also the first of the great "encounters" in which El Greco brought one world face to face with another. The composition is two-storied: above, Christ surrounded by angels, standing on the Book of the Gospels, trampling Death and a dark demon underfoot, and crowning an armored saint, warrior or king; below, the theological virtues hold the foreground, while on the right the gaping Jaws of Hell engulf the Damned and the procession of the Elect winds away in the distance. Painted fifteen years later (the *Last Judgment* mentioned earlier holding an intermediary position between these two works), the *Adoration of the Name of Jesus* at the Escorial (traditionally known as *The Dream of Philip II*) reverts to some of the key motifs of that early work, but handles them with greater skill and loftiness. The picture illustrates a passage from The Epistle of Paul to the Philippians: "That at the name of Jesus every knee should bow, of things in heaven, and things in earth, and things under the earth." In it Christ's monogram alone occupies the place of honor, shining brilliantly amidst the angelic host. The three worlds unfold successively on a single, almost horizontal plane, with Philip II kneeling between the Church Militant and the Jaws

◄ HELL, DETAIL OF THE ADORATION OF THE NAME OF JESUS, C. 1580.

DETAIL OF THE MARTYRDOM OF ST MAURICE.

THE STONING OF ST STEPHEN, DETAIL OF THE BURIAL OF COUNT ORGAZ. ▶

of Hell. Wearing black gloves and dressed in black except for his white ruffs, the king forms the only dark spot in a brilliant canvas, whose glittering colors are franker and freer than in any other work by El Greco.

Then came *The Martyrdom of St Maurice*, in which there is no minimizing the essential part played by the open heavens

and the bright lights that rain down with the chorus of angels bearing crowns for the army of naked martyrs hastening to death so willingly that already they resemble a procession of ghosts fading into the depths of the picture. But there is also a curious miniature recently discovered in the Colegio del Patriarca at Valencia, mention of which, moreover, is found in inventories dating back to the end of the 17th century: *The Dream of St Martin*, as he lies at the foot of a column while the apparition of Christ flanked by angels fills the heavens. This work, by no means unworthy of El Greco, bears the date of 1582. As for the upper, the "celestial" half of *The Burial of Count Orgaz*, long disparaged by the majority of critics, the unreality of the scene is obvious, but so is its perfect spiritual coherence in conjunction with the rest of the picture, for it alone gives full significance to the scene below, which without it—as is sufficiently clear from the partial copy at the Prado— appears cramped and in want of air. The architectural coherence of the two scenes is no less a fact; the extreme elongation of the two intercessors, the Virgin and St John the Baptist, serves to pillar up the terminal arches and is structurally necessary to the balance of the masses. A little more "disturbing" perhaps is a detail in the lower scene: the Stoning of St Stephen painted on the gorgeous chasuble of the saint, a vivid sketch of considerable violence which, though no bigger than a miniature, is "visionary" in the full sense of the word, with the greenish sky, the dim landscape sown with mysterious buildings, and above all the phantasmal executioners and the hot streaks of pigment that model their tawny backs.

From now on El Greco drew steadily away from the semi-realism of his early years in Spain. Never again did he juxtapose two worlds. Instead, he elaborated a world of his own imagining, either reverting to earlier themes and recasting them or seizing outright on fresh themes hitherto unexploited.

As far as we can judge from the extant works, El Greco now felt a renewed interest in subjects which he had already interpreted many years before in Italy, but which he had left untouched in Spain. Turning to three such themes already treated in the *Modena Polyptych—The Adoration of the Shepherds, The Annunciation, The Baptism of Christ*—he made a new version of each. He again painted *Christ driving the Traders from the Temple*, of which there exist several versions made in Italy. A comparison of his unusually numerous *Annunciations* is instructive: the earliest, the Modena *Annunciation*, issues directly from Titian and Tintoretto, with the angel almost flush with the floor in a slightly terraced vestibule, and with, behind the angel, a deeply receding passageway; the only novelty in the Prado *Annunciation*, which he may have brought with him to Spain from Italy, is the distinctly Roman profile of the angel and the toga-like tunic draped over him in the manner of the ancients. Then the theme disappears altogether for many years, only to reappear in a double series of *Annunciations* devoid of spatial depth and bathed in a strange light. Those showing only the Virgin and the angel (Hospice of Illescas, Budapest Museum, Zuloaga Museum) draw the two figures closer together, with the angel overhanging Mary in such a way as to suggest a long, linking, serpentine line. In the other set (Bilbao Museum, Museo Balaguer at Villanueva y Geltrú) the height and depth of the scene are vastly increased and an orchestra of angel musicians hovers in the clouds above the Virgin's chamber without walls. The actual episode of the Annunciation is swept up in a whirl of gyrating, intermingling colors; the figures, modeled in spurts and trailing wisps of light, linger in the mind less as human forms than as large patches of bright color.

PAGE 98: THE CRUCIFIXION, C. 1590-1595.
PAGE 99: THE RESURRECTION, C. 1590-1595.

98

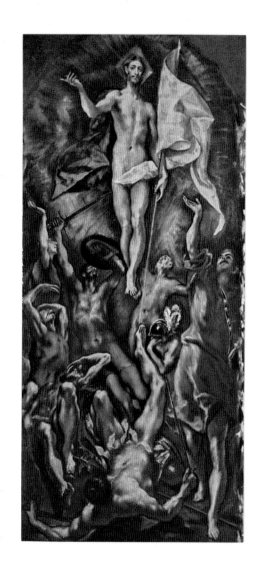

Christ driving the Traders from the Temple is a theme that requires very different treatment since it necessarily marshals a host of figures in an architectural setting that cannot be omitted. Here the loose breadth and scattered figure group of the Italian versions gave way to a new rhythmic concentration and a tight-knit composition cut low at the top. In the later versions now in Boston Museum and the Frick Collection every secondary figure that could possibly go has been ruthlessly eliminated; all that remains is a fan-shaped swirl of naked bodies falling back under the lashing whip of a tall, wrathful, prancing figure steeped in light. But in the canvas preserved in the church of San Ginès in Madrid, which may be taken as El Greco's final conception of this theme, the large figure group fills no more than the lower half of the picture, which has grown considerably higher and shallower; substituted for the spacious, arcaded temple is now a grand but well-confined tabernacle in the pure style of antiquity with a nude statue towering in a niche above the main scene. A somber, solemn light floats motionlessly above the heads, glistening on stately columns, while faces, bare legs and folds of garments glow through the gloaming of the foreground.

New themes arise parallel to the old: *The Feast in the House of Simon* (Art Institute of Chicago) in which a similar architectural setting solemnizes the circle of wonderstruck apostles; several versions of *Christ in the Garden of Olives* (Lille Museum, National Gallery, London, Herzog Collection, Budapest), all fantastically lit up by beams of light which, fingering the bushes and illuminating the group of soldiers in the background, are —far more than the rather expressionless Christ—the essential agents of a dramatic scene rendered doubly fantastic by the eery dug-out in which—either above or below Christ, depending on the version—the dozing apostles lie in an undersea haze of gloom-ridden light. There is also *The Coronation of the Virgin*,

DETAIL OF THE VISION OF THE APOCALYPSE, C. 1610.

a theme treated in several versions whose central figure group may have been inspired by Dürer or by Taddeo Zuccaro, whose color and atmosphere, however, are entirely El Greco's. Contrary to what we might expect, it is the earliest version (in the parish church of Talavera la Vieja) that is built up vertically so as to include a chorus of enraptured saints gazing up at the wonder of the Coronation. The late versions (in the Prado and at Illescas) are purely celestial scenes; the earth having fallen away, all that is left are great patches of golden white, carmine and keen blues among great icebergs of cloud shot through with shafts of light.

THE LAOCOON, C. 1610-1614. (BEFORE CLEANING)

THE LAOCOON, C. 1610-1614.

The celebrated marble group of the Laocoön, a work of the Rhodian sculptors of the 1st century B.C., discovered in Rome in 1506, was copied by Alonso Berruguete before being interpreted by El Greco, whose treatment on the whole remains Michelangelesque. It is a curious coincidence that Spanish decorum insisted on having several figures draped, just as papal decorum had insisted on clothing certain figures in Michelangelo's Sistine frescos. Reproduced above, for the first time, is the original version as it now stands after a recent cleaning which revealed a third standing figure on the right. On the opposite page: the same picture before cleaning.

Datable to some time shortly before his death are two of his most wonderful creations: *The Vision of Apocalypse* and *The Death of Laocoön*. Whether pagan or Christian, the inspiration of both expresses the mystery and awe of man overcome by the powers of heaven. Both works are alike too in the gigantic proportions of the leading figures, treated like statues and distinguished by

VIEW OF TOLEDO, C. 1605-1610.

◄   VIEW OF TOLEDO, DETAIL OF THE LAOCOON, C. 1610-1614.

a kind of autumnal recollection of Italian humanism embodied in the sublimated nudity of human forms. The first (Zuloaga Museum, Zumaya) must have formed part of one of the commissions given El Greco by the Hospice of San Juan Bautista. Unfortunately the upper half of the picture having disappeared, it is impossible to say exactly what the subject of the remaining portion is. It has long been known as *Sacred and Profane Love*, but this title fails to make sense. Have we here the illustration of a passage in the Book of Revelation (perhaps the Opening of the Fifth Seal, with the souls of the Just, "of them that were slain for the word of God," demanding vengeance), or simply a general vision of the Resurrection? No matter. The contrast between the somber luster of the monumental St John on the left, with his panic gesture, and the tall, willowy nudes, their lissome bodies gleaming with light, is more than enough to evoke a powerful emotional response.

As for *Laocoön* (National Gallery, Washington), we may take it to be the work which the artist jealously kept in his studio unseen and which figured on the inventory drawn up at his death. Whatever its sources (antique sculpture or Renaissance prints, the names of Jean de Gourmont and Fontana having been suggested in connection with the latter), El Greco's interpretation resembles no other. The leading figures are drawn apart rather than drawn taut; their lithe bodies are like the scattered columns of a temple burst asunder; yet they are linked by a skillful counterpoint of inverted curves. Their massive forms stand out against a vast panorama which is Troy in the obvious guise of Toledo.

At more or less the same period El Greco twice painted "portraits" of his adopted city. The great panoramic view (in the El Greco Museum, Toledo) is less impressive at first

THE ASSUMPTION, C. 1610. ▶

sight than the small partial view in the Metropolitan Museum, which shows very distinctly the Alcántara Bridge, the Alcázar and the cathedral beneath a raging thunderstorm, and which, green-hued and lightning-streaked, is the only landscape in the modern sense of the word to be found in El Greco's œuvre. Yet the panoramic view painted in a refreshing scale of near-pink ochres and russet greens, with patches of pale blue sky, is the most "impressionistic" Greco imaginable; it is a remarkable fact that the youth holding out the plan of the city is drawn without contour-lines, his person built up in gradations of green pigment. It is also the picture which most naturally and fitly unites an extreme precision of detail—both in the plan of the city and the buildings themselves—with a full measure of poetic license in its blend of humanism and Christianity: the Tagus personified by a river god, the Virgin with her angels suspended in mid-air long enough to remit a chasuble to her faithful paladin St Ildefonso, and above all the astonishing liberty El Greco took in substituting his own order for nature's and squarely swinging round the Hospice of San Juan Bautista so as to bring the fine façade into full view in the center of the composition.

All this is much like a pictorial counterpart of Góngora, with the mythological extravagance of his *Polifemo* and the almost magic battery of his hyperboles, ellipses and cold paroxysms. But any attempt to read a philosophic system into his well-regulated pictorial organization is foredoomed, though it is a fact that his world, as he grew older, increasingly diverged from the common-sense world most men swear by. Even more than the apparent whimsy with which he proportioned figures and things, it is the cast-iron unity of a picture space devoid of atmosphere—or steeped, rather, in something like the atmosphere of a diving bell—which intrigues and baffles us,

◀ THE PENTECOST, C. 1605-1610.

as we see heaven and earth flooded with the same light that floods purgatory. It is also the leveling of differences from man to man, the repertory of haggard expressions and ecstatic gestures increasingly scaled down and intensified, the schematization of silhouettes, which end up as huge insubstantial puppets. This is a world doomed to disintegration, and for a long time the explanation was thought to be medical or pathological in nature. The Portuguese mental specialist Ricardo Jorge transferred to the artist himself the signs of degeneration and maniac insanity which he felt were perceptible in his models; but this is refuted by the accounts of contemporaries such as Pacheco, to whom, though he was well aware of El Greco's eccentricities, it never occurred to treat him as a madman, and who, on the contrary, respectfully acknowledged him to be a "great philosopher" and an erudite theoretician in all matters touching his art. Then there are those who would have us believe that El Greco suffered from astigmatism; but how account for the fact that, even in his most capricious works, he could paint the branch of a tree, a vase, or a bouquet of flowers with all the precision and loving care of a soft-hearted realist? No one can any longer credit such explanations as these. Besides, several more recent medical diagnoses are much more subtle and circumspect. Dr Marañon has suggested that the painter's imagination may have fed for years on the same model, presumably someone in an asthenic, hyperthyroid condition whose fits of depression alternated with periods of exalted dynamism. Dr Perera has likened El Greco's images to those described by hashish eaters after their intoxicating visions. These are ingenious ideas certainly, but it may be questioned whether they are really needed to "explain" El Greco.

Compelled in old age to fall back upon himself, upon his paintings, his books, his memories and dreams, perhaps El Greco gave himself up to a kind of "quest of the absolute." A subtle, far-ranging mind suckled on Hellenic idealism, initiated in Italy into the quasi-religious mysteries of Renaissance science, and a believer for whom this world can only be momentary exile from the Christian paradise—certainly this combination of spiritual forces admirably prepared the man for just such a quest. Why not read into his art the age-old dream of a union of mind and matter, when that art is so manifestly shy of all that is neuter and lifeless? Just as he used sculptor's figurines the better to grasp forms modeled in light, so he may also have used mirrors and lenses to learn the art of exaggerating contrasts and differences of proportion between planes in order to deepen the expression and life-force of his master figures. Perhaps insufficient attention has been paid the observations of Elie Lambert, who compared El Greco's compositions to photographs taken with a short-focus lens when the operator has failed to place all his objects equidistant from the camera.

As an architect, it was only natural for him to elongate or contract figures according to the position assigned them in the composition as a whole, according above all as they were meant to be viewed along a higher or lower angle of vision—and only natural for him to subordinate them to the geometrical pattern which is the very framework of the picture. As a Platonist and a Christian (and as an assiduous reader of the *Dialogues* of Francesco Patrizzi, an Italianized Greek, the only philosopher of his time whose works figured in his library), may he not have dreamed of transposing the old theory of light as renewed by St Basil and the medieval doctors of the church, of bathing his canvases in *lumen*—that inner, incorporeal light which flows everywhere inexhaustibly and is the manifestation of that vital energy which lies at the origin of life and movement—and eliminating mere *lux*, the light we perceive, which illuminates earthly bodies? As a musician (for music is an essential feature of his work, the best example being the charming groups of angels bearing harps, viols and theorbos, such as that above the *Annunciation* formerly owned by the Marquis of Urquijo and now in America), may he not have dreamed of abolishing the frontier between the arts of space and the arts of time, of recording musical emotions in terms of rhythms of line and color? Everything in his last works points to such dreams as these—in *The Pentecost* (Prado), in which, as if borne aloft by a giant's breath, Virgin and apostles flicker and fuse like the licking flames of a chimney fire; in the long, wavy, translucent figures of *The Marriage of the Virgin* (Bucarest); and above all in the two paintings made for San Vicente: *The Visitation* (now at Dumbarton Oaks), an architecture of illuminated bodies so powerfully self-sufficing that they have no need of faces; and *The Assumption* (San Vicente Museum, Toledo), a radiant spiral linking the sky to the hills of Toledo and dipping down to link the bouquet of flowers of the fields to the dove of the Holy Ghost, of which Maurice Barrès wrote: "It is like a voice, a song that trembles in the air, or rather like a thing at rest after the dance of life." El Greco himself might have accepted these words as a definition of the goal he glimpsed at his journey's end.

EL GRECO IN OUR TIME

THE VISITATION, C. 1610.

EL GRECO IN OUR TIME

EL GRECO's posthumous fate was as strange as the course of his life. Remembered and highly esteemed well into the second half of the 17th century, though followed by no genuine disciples (his true posterity is to be found in certain works of Velazquez and in a few of Goya's last portraits), he thereafter gradually sank into oblivion. His fate in many ways resembles that of Georges de La Tour, who also enjoyed a great reputation in his lifetime. But La Tour was left in complete and peaceful neglect for nearly three centuries, while El Greco became the scapegoat of the neo-classical critics who liked to point him out as a prime example of the wreck of a great talent when it fails to abide by the hallowed principles of "true art."

When at last the 19th-century Romantics began exhuming the treasures of Spanish painting, it was El Greco who bene-fitted least. For some reason he languished in a state of semi-disgrace and only the English showed anything more than a half-hearted interest in him. Even Théophile Gautier, his usual insight failing him, saw nothing in the paintings at the Hospice of San Juan Bautista but "depraved energy and morbid forces betraying a great painter and a madman of genius." Visitors to the Louvre had no eye for the eight Grecos in Louis Philippe's Spanish Gallery and some of the best of them passed into the collection of the King of Rumania. Only an aristocracy of poets, artists and independent critics showed any curiosity in this "ostracized" artist whose genius they divined, though they knew almost nothing about him. Among these men were Delacroix, Baudelaire, Millet, Degas, Théodore Duret and Zacharie Astruc; the latter, keenly enthusiastic, opened Manet's eyes to El Greco. Cézanne was attracted to him early in his career, though he knew him only at second hand, copying *The Woman with a Fur* from a print in a popular magazine of the day.

El Greco's hour of triumph was not to come until early in the 20th century. It can be dated to 1902 when the very first exhibition of his works took place at the Prado.

Two Spanish painters who lived in Paris around the turn of the century—the Catalan Santiago Rusiñol and the Basque Ignacio Zuloaga, a shrewd and impassioned collector—greatly stimulated interest in El Greco both in France and Spain. One result was that in 1910 the French novelist Maurice Barrès published his *Greco, ou le secret de Tolède*, a major contribution to the rehabilitation of the painter and a book which may still be read with profit by students of El Greco. If we disregard a few historical inaccuracies, a few prejudices typical of aesthetes of that day, and too systematic an identification of El Greco with 16th-century Toledo, it remains one of the most penetrating studies of him ever written, and contains some of Barrès' finest pages. This book launched a tradition in modern French letters; since then such widely different writers as Jean Cassou, Eugène Dabit and Jean Cocteau have sung the praises of El Greco with the same zealous conviction.

The vogue for El Greco is not a passing fashion. It is, rather, one of the key episodes in the pictorial and spiritual upheaval of our time.

Impressionism cleared the way for this revision of values by lifting painting, once and for all, from the plane of mere anecdote to that of poetic creation. But it took the triumvirate of Van Gogh, Gauguin and Cézanne, with their exaltation of color, their cult of expressive violence, their subordination of forms to rhythmic power, to posit El Greco as the most brilliant and proficient of their precursors.

Since then El Greco's influence has shared the fortunes of Cézanne's influence, acting powerfully on each generation of painters. The Fauves looked to him for his paroxysmal handling of color and form, the Cubists for his reconstruction of the picture space *more geometrico*, the Surrealists for his systematic incursions into a dreamworld. Today he enjoys a popularity with the public at large which few other Old Masters can rival.

His fame has reached a higher point now than ever before and has settled there to stay. Sought after by the museums of the entire world, which outbid one another for his canvases, brought before an ever wider public by illustrated art books

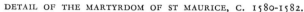

DETAIL OF THE MARTYRDOM OF ST MAURICE, C. 1580-1582.

and guide books, and mustered at last into the front rank of the world's artists in every history of art, El Greco throws a spell over "solitary souls" that does not easily wear off. His paintings have lost none of their force and freshness, for he tackled three centuries ago the very problems that impassion present-day artists, and he solved them in a way that is all his own. That union of genuine religious emotion with bold speculations increasingly abstract, increasingly inspired, that union of the gorgeous and the stark—no master of modern art has re-discovered its secret. And among all the masters of the past, the spiritual ventures of none tease and excite the mind so much as those El Greco embarked upon when, like a conquistador of the arts, he ranged beyond the accepted limits of painting into the unknown.

DOCUMENTARY MATERIAL

BIOGRAPHICAL NOTICES

SELECTED BIBLIOGRAPHY

INDEX OF NAMES

LIST OF COLORPLATES

TABLE OF CONTENTS

DOCUMENTARY MATERIAL

EL GRECO AS SEEN BY HIS CONTEMPORARIES

To Cardinal Farnese at Viterbo.

There has just arrived in Rome a young Candiot, pupil of Titian, who in my opinion ranks among the most excellent in painting. Amongst other things he has made a portrait of himself which has much amazed all the painters of Rome. I should desire to place him under the protection of your Lordship, though no more is required for his livelihood than temporary accommodations at the Farnese Palace, till such time as he makes his own way in Rome. I therefore earnestly beseech and beg your Lordship to instruct Ludovico, your Lordship's steward, to provide him with any available room in the garret of the Palace. Your most illustrious and reverend Lordship would thereby accomplish an act of virtue and charity in every way worthy of your Lordship, to whom I should be much obliged and to whom I reverently pay my most dutiful respects.

Your Lordship's very humble servant

DON GIULIO CLOVIO

(Letter dated November 16, 1570, from the *Carteggio farnesiano*. First published by Ronchini in *Atti e memorie della RR. Diputazione di Storia Patria III*, Modena 1865.)

... During the pontificate of the late Pius V, of blessed memory, there came to Rome he who was commonly known as Il Greco. Having worked in Venice and studied in especial the works of Titian, he had attained to high mastery in his profession. He came from Venice to Rome at a time when painters were not plentiful, and the works of those that there were failed to display the resoluteness and the freshness that characterized his own. His ardent spirit was stirred up even more by numerous commissions, amongst which may be cited the picture which is at present in the possession of the advocate Lancilotti, and which is taken by many to be a Titian. At that time the figures in Michelangelo's *Last Judgment* which the Pope held to be indecent were being covered over. He ventured to say that, should the entire work be destroyed, he would take it upon him to do all of it over again with propriety and seemliness and to make it withal a piece of painting no less fine.

His views in the matter incensed all the painters and lovers of painting there, and he was obliged to leave for Spain where, under Philip II, he painted many fine works of excellent taste. But with the coming of

Pellegrino da Bologna, Federico Zuccaro and sundry Flemings who, by their art and their wiles, occupied the front rank, he resolved to quit the Court and to withdraw to Toledo, where he died at an advanced age, having by then virtually abandoned his art. When all is said and done, he was a man who in his maturity was worthy of a place amongst the best of his century.

GIULIO CESARE MANCINI
1614-1619, MS. Biblioteca Vaticana.
(First published by Roberto Longhi
in *L'Arte*, 1914.)

... Of one Dominico Greco, who is still alive and still doing excellent things at Toledo, there has here remained a picture of St Maurice and his warriors which he made for the altar of that saint. It failed to find favor with His Majesty, which is natural enough, for it finds favor with few people, though some say that it is a highly deserving work, that its maker is very skilled, and that excellent things are to be seen by his hand. In this opinions and tastes contend with one another. It seems to me that the difference between things made with reason and art and things made without them is that the former satisfy everyone and the latter only a few. For art does nothing else but correspond with reason and nature, whose imprint all minds bear. Whatever is ill-made, behind whatever appearance or gloss it be, may deceive the ignorant and thus satisfy the ignorant and those who do not consider thoughtfully. After all, as our Mute well demonstrated—Juan Fernández Navarrete, called the Mute—saints should be painted in such a way that, instead of removing our desire to pray before them, they inspire us with worship, for the chief effect of painting and its end are nothing else but that.

FRAY JOSÉ DE SIGUENZA
(*Historia de la Orden de San Jerónimo*,
1600-1605. IV, 17.)

Concerning *The Burial of Count Orgaz*:

... The painting was executed, and it is one of the very finest in all Spain. Men come from foreign lands to see it with especial admiration; and the people of Toledo, far from tiring of it, continually find in it new matter to gaze at. In it may be seen indeed, realistically portrayed, many of the illustrious men of our time. Its maker was the painter Domingo de Theotocopuli, by birth a Greek.

FRANCISCO DE PISA
(*Apuntamientos...*, manuscript
of a History of Toledo, 1612.)

Many painters of prowess hold beauty and suavity cheap, but not "relief." So with Bassano, Michelangelo, Caravaggio and our own Jusepe de Ribera. And we may also number amongst them Dominico Greco; for though we have contested at various times certain of his judgments and paradoxes, we cannot exclude him from the ranks of the great painters when we see certain things by his hand so lively and vigorous (in a style of his own) that they match those of the greatest men...

... The ancients were not alone in their erudition. In our century too there have been learned men, not only in painting but also in the humanities. Thus Michelangelo, of whom we may read many compositions in verse, thus Leonardo da Vinci, Bronzino, Giorgio Vasari; thus Dominico Greco, who was an eminent philosopher, full of subtle observations, and who wrote on painting...

... Dominico Greco in the year 1611 showed me an entire cupboard filled with earthenware models, made by his own hand to be used for his works, and—what exceeds admiration—the originals of all his pictures, painted in oil on a small scale, in a large room which, at his behest, his son let me see.

... Who would believe that Dominico Greco so often went back to his paintings, and retouched them again and again, only to leave the colors distinct and unblended and to give them the look of brutal sketches, like an affectation of vigor...

... I was much amazed when I asked Dominico Greco in the year 1611 which was the most difficult, whether the color or the drawing, and he replied: the color. And still more amazing was to hear him speak with so little respect of Michelangelo—the Father of painting—, saying that he was a worthy man, but that he never learnt how to paint. Furthermore, for whosoever knows the man, it is not surprising to see him depart from the common sentiment of artists, for he was as singular in all else as he was in his painting.

FRANCISCO PACHECO
(*Arte de la Pintura, 1649.*)

About the same time there came from Italy a painter called Dominico Greco, said to have been a pupil of Titian. He made his home in the very ancient and illustrious city of Toledo, where he introduced a manner so extravagant that to this day nothing so fanciful has been seen. And the best connoisseurs would be hard put to imagine his extravagance, for such is the discordance between his works that they do not look to be by the same hand. He came to this city with a great reputation, so great that it was given to be understood that nothing in the world was superior to his works. And, in very truth, some are worthy of the highest esteem and capable of ranking him amongst the most famous painters. His character is as extravagant as his painting. It has never been heard said that he ever made a contract for any of his works, for to his mind no price was high enough to pay for them... He earned much money, but he spent it lavishly in maintaining a style of living luxurious in the extreme, indeed he went so far as to keep musicians in his hire to soothe and distract him whilst he took his meals. He worked a great deal and the sole wealth he bequeathed at his death were two hundred unfinished pictures. He reached an advanced age, ever enjoying the same esteem and repute. He was a famous architect and very eloquent of speech. He had few pupils, for few were minded to follow his doctrines, so fanciful and extravagant that they were suited only to himself...

JUSEPE MARTÍNEZ

*(Discursos practicables del nobilisimo arte
de la pintura, 1673.)*

BIOGRAPHICAL NOTICES

ON THE PRINCIPAL CONTEMPORARIES OF EL GRECO

CASTILLA, DIEGO (1508-1584) AND LUIS DE (1536-after 1615)

Churchmen and humanists, patrons of El Greco at various times, these two Toledan notables were descendants of a natural son of the famous king of Castile, Peter the Cruel. They were born of different wives of their father, which explains the great age difference between them (28 years). Dean of Toledo Cathedral, Diego was already an old man when El Greco arrived in Spain. He was the testamentary executor of a Portuguese lady named Doña Maria de Silva, the childless widow of a dignitary at the Court of Charles V, who had withdrawn to the convent of Santo Domingo el Antiguo, and it was in fulfillment of her last wishes that he began renovating the church in 1577 and thus called on Herrera, El Greco and Monegro for their collaboration. He died a few years later, in 1584.

His half-brother Luis, born in 1536, accompanied Pedro Chacón to Rome in 1570 and there moved in the circle of humanists whose guiding spirit was Fulvio Orsini. Having made the acquaintance of El Greco, he recommended him to his brother upon his return to Spain. Appointed Dean of Cuenca Cathedral in 1575, he nevertheless remained in close touch with El Greco and his family. Executor of the painter's will, he commissioned an altarpiece from Jorge Manuel in 1615, a year after El Greco's death.

CEVALLOS, JERÓNIMO DE (1559-AFTER 1623)

Born at Escalona, near Toledo, he was one of the most renowned Toledan jurists of the 16th century. He wrote a number of treatises on legal and political questions, and was also a member of the Municipal Council of Toledo.

CHACÓN, PEDRO (1526-1581)

A humanist of considerable standing in Toledo, he accompanied the archbishop of Seville on a journey to Rome in 1570, remained there, became friendly with Fulvio Orsini and gained a great reputation as an expert on numismatics and glyptics. He died in Rome in 1581.

CLOVIO, GIORGIO GIULIO (1498-1578)

Italian painter and miniaturist, a Croat by birth, his original name being Glovichitch. Employed by the great Venetian family of the Grimani, he accompanied Cardinal Grimani to Rome and worked in the studio of

Giulio Romano. In 1524 he accompanied the Cardinal on a journey to Hungary. Maltreated and imprisoned during the sack of Rome in 1527, he took refuge at Mantua, then lived for some years at Perugia. In 1540 he entered the service of Cardinal Farnese. As a miniature-painter he was famous throughout Europe, being known as the "miniature Michelangelo." His best illuminated manuscripts (*Breviary, Divine Comedy, Lives of the Dukes of Urbino* in the Vatican Library) are stamped with the immediate influence of Michelangelo. Age and ill-health prevented him from accepting the invitation of Philip II to come to Spain in 1572. He died in Rome in 1578.

COVARRUBIAS Y LEYVA, DIEGO (1512-1577) AND ANTONIO (1514-1602)

Sons of Alonso de Covarrubias—"master of works" at Toledo Cathedral and architect to the Emperor Charles V, renovator of the Alcázars of Toledo and Madrid and one of the leading figures of the classical Renaissance in Spain—these two brothers, natives of Toledo, ranked among the outstanding jurists and theologians of the 16th century. Diego, the elder, was professor of canon law at the University of Salamanca, then bishop of Segovia. He played an important part in the Council of Trent, helping to draft the decrees of reform. He was a member of the Council of Castile, which he presided from 1574 to 1577, when he died in Madrid.

Antonio, the younger brother, after accompanying Diego to the Council of Trent, became canon of Toledo and a member of the Council of Castile. His reputation as a Hellenist and archeologist matched his renown as a jurist. He was one of El Greco's closest friends in Toledo.

GÓNGORA, LUIS DE ARGOTE Y (1561-1627)

Spain's greatest baroque poet, Góngora came of an aristocratic family of Cordova. After studying civil and canon law at the University of Salamanca, he obtained a minor clerical post at Cordova Cathedral, his functions taking him on many journeys and missions throughout Spain. Ordained priest about 1606 and appointed honorary Chaplain to King Philip III in 1617, he thereafter resided in Madrid, only returning to Cordova in 1626, where he died in the following year. Though no collected edition of his poems was published till after his death (by Hozes in 1633) he was already famous at the age of twenty-five for his sonnets, ballads, satires and *letrillas*, whose polished refinement yet retained all the vigor of the popular tradition. The larger poems of his maturity—the *Fábula de Polifemo y Galatea* (1612) and the *Soledades* (1613)—show that high elaboration of style with which his name is associated; with their unusual metaphors and systematic transposition of sounds, they prove Góngora to have been a precursor of the style created by Mallarmé two and a half centuries later.

LA FUENTE, RODRIGO DE (1510-1589)

A skilled Toledan physician with a great reputation, he was also an eminent scholar and humanist. He wrote an elegant Latin poem which took first prize (an emerald ring) in a literary contest in 1587.

MONEGRO, JUAN BAUTISTA (C. 1545-1621)

Born of a family of stonecutters in northern Spain (at Monegro in the Santander mountains), he is mentioned as being at Toledo in 1568, where he married and worked as a sculptor. Between 1572 and 1583, he was several times invited to the Escorial where, among other things, he made the statues of the Kings of Judah on the façade of the church. At Toledo in 1577 he was commissioned to build the altarpieces designed for Santo Domingo el Antiguo by El Greco (with whom he never got on very well and whose plans he distorted to some extent). He decorated several gates and bridges of the city and directed various building projects in the churches of Toledo and vicinity (notably at the monastery of Guadalupe), always in a severely classical style. His greatest work is the large chapel of the Virgen del Sagrario in Toledo Cathedral (1608-1616). Highly esteemed by Philip II who made him architect of the Alcázar, he was also appointed building supervisor of the Cathedral in 1606. He died in Toledo in 1621.

NIÑO DE GUEVARA, FERNANDO (1541-1609)

Scion of an aristocratic family of Toledo, he occupied a number of important administrative posts (rising to the Chancellorship of Granada) until, at the personal request of Philip II, he was appointed Cardinal by Pope Clement VIII. After three years in Rome, he returned to Spain in 1599 as Inquisitor General. At Toledo in 1600 he presided over an auto-da-fé at which the king and queen were present. Appointed archbishop of Seville in 1601, he died there in 1609.

ORRENTE, PEDRO (C. 1570-1643)

Spanish painter born about 1570 at Montealegre (province of Murcia), he seems to have been schooled at Toledo and might have been a pupil of El Greco. In any case he is known to have been a close friend of Jorge Manuel. He worked chiefly at Valencia, where he struck out in the direction of tenebrist realism (notably in his masterpiece, the large *St Sebastian* in Valencia Cathedral). He seems to have been highly successful with biblical and pastoral themes (*The Sacrifice of Isaac, Jacob and Laban*, etc.) treated as genre scenes and nightpieces in the manner of Jacopo Bassano. He died at Valencia in 1643.

ORSINI, FULVIO (1529-1600)

Coming of a great Roman family whose fortunes were then on the wane, he was luckily taken up by Canon Delfini who gave him a thorough grounding in Hellenism and archeology. Canon of St John Lateran in 1554, he entered the service of the Farneses and was librarian to Cardinals Ranuccio, Alessandro and Odoardo Farnese in turn. For forty years he enjoyed their confidence and trust, directing the decoration of their palace. Scholar, bibliophile and numismatist, he played host to innumerable Italian and foreign humanists and corresponded regularly with writers and scholars all over Europe. His unrivaled collection of books passed into the Vatican Library at his death in 1600.

PACHECO, FRANCISCO (1564-1654)

Born at Sanlúcar de Barrameda, then a flourishing port at the mouth of the Guadalquivir, Pacheco came of a family of mariners but, drawn to letters at an early age, he was raised by his uncle, canon of Seville Cathedral and a well-known humanist. Alongside his literary studies, he studied painting with Luis Fernández. After making a trip to Flanders, he settled down in Seville where he quickly made a name for himself as a painter, his studio becoming a haunt of artists and scholars. He thereafter left Seville only twice, making two trips to Madrid: in 1611—when he called on El Greco on his way through Toledo—and in 1623-1624. His great pupil was Velazquez, who in 1618 married his only daughter. Living to a ripe old age, Pacheco formed the link between 16th and 17th century Spanish painting, though he remained essentially a mannerist, and a mannerist colder and more shrinking than most; even his venture into realism in the early years of the 17th century (e.g. *The Life of St Peter Nolasco* in the Museo Provincial, Seville) remains very faint-hearted. Doomed to mediocrity as a painter and poet, he was none the less a firstrate teacher and, above all, an invaluable chronicler of the Spain of his day. His *Libro de verdaderos retratos*, begun in 1599, is a gallery of the famous men of Seville. His *Arte de la pintura* (first published in 1649) is a triple compendium of contemporary aesthetics, painting techniques (including the polychroming of statuary) and Christian iconography (the Holy Office of the Inquisition having charged him with the task of investigating the orthodoxy of all works of art then being produced in Spain).

PARAVICINO, FRAY HORTENSIO FÉLIX DE (1580-1633)

Born in Madrid of a family hailing originally from Milan. At the age of twenty he joined the Trinitarians, a religious order devoted to the ransoming of Christian captives (it was this order that liberated Cervantes after his capture by Barbary corsairs). His eloquent preaching soon brought him into notice, in particular a sermon pronounced before King Philip III at Salamanca in 1605. Named to high posts in the order, entrusted with missions abroad, appointed royal preacher in 1616, admired and praised by Lope de Vega and Quevedo, he was the great baroque orator of Spain's Golden Age. His *Oraciones evangélicas* was published posthumously in 1638. His devout and secular poems (among them four sonnets to El Greco) appeared in 1641 under the title *Obras póstumas, divinas y humanas*.

PATRIZZI, FRANCESCO (1529-1597)

Born in Dalmatia of a family in humble circumstances, he had to fend for himself from earliest youth, taking service under successive masters with whom he visited France, Spain and Greece. Then he gained the patronage of the Venetian bishop of Cyprus, Mocenigo, who enabled him to complete his studies at Padua. After teaching for seventeen years at Ferrara, where the duke created the chair of philosophy especially for him, he was invited to Rome by Pope Clement VIII and there spent the rest of his life. He published many works on science, rhetoric, aesthetics, the art of war and, above all, metaphysics, combating Aristotle and developing a mystical, neo-Platonic philosophy tinged with Egyptian and Persian ideas, in which light is taken as the synthesis and expression of godhead. Two of his works figure in the inventory of El Greco's library: *La milizia romana* (1583) and *Della retorica, dieci dialoghi* (1562).

PISA, FRANCISCO DE (1533-1616)

This Toledan priest was a prolific writer on many subjects. Famous in his day as a theologian and commentator of Aristotle, he is chiefly interesting today for his historical writings. In 1605 he published a *Descripción de la imperial Ciudad de Toledo e historia de sus antiguedades y grandezas y cosas memorables que en ella han acontecido*, which is a mine of precious information. He became canon of Segovia Cathedral and upon his death left the manuscript of a sequel (still unpublished) to the above work.

PREBOSTE, FRANCISCO DE (1554-?)

The faithful factotum and collaborator of El Greco, Preboste seems to have been closely attached to his master's household. Yet all we know about the man is contained in the notes published by F.B. de San Román on the basis of documents in the archives of Toledo. An Italian born in 1554, he presumably accompanied El Greco to Spain, where his name is frequently coupled with that of his master, who empowered him to sign contracts and receive payments. After May 1607 Jorge Manuel assumed these duties and no further mention of Preboste is to be found. Did he quarrel with El Greco? Did he meet his death in the course of one of his many business trips? The mystery remains unsolved.

QUIROGA, GASPAR DE (1499-1593)

Born at Madrigal de las Altas Torres (near Avila), canon of Toledo,
then bishop of Cuenca, he was singled out by Philip II for his allegiance
to the Crown in all religious questions. Entrusted with foreign missions,
appointed Inquisitor General in 1572, he obtained the archbishopric of
Toledo at the age of nearly eighty through the good offices of his close
friend Antonio Perez, then the favorite minister of Philip II. Austere,
upright and hard-working, he held his post up to his death in 1593.

ROMERO, CAPTAIN JULIAN (1518-1577)

Famous soldier and knight of St James, he took a leading part in the
Duke of Alba's Italian and Flemish campaigns, where his exploits won
him the nickname "El de las hazañas" (the man of valorous deeds). He died
in Italy, near Cremona, in 1577.

TAVERA, JUAN (1472-1545)

Not only a scholarly humanist and patron of the arts, Cardinal Tavera
was one of the most distinguished Spanish diplomats and administrators
in the reign of the Emperor Charles V. From bishop of Burgo de Osma
and archbishop of Compostella, he became president of the Council of
Castile, which, at the personal behest of Charles V, he continued to preside
for several years after his elevation to the archbishopric of Toledo. Following the example of his predecessor Cardinal Mendoza, founder of the great
Hospital de Santa Cruz, he founded (in 1541) the Hospital de San Juan
Bautista at Toledo which is better known today as the Hospital Tavera.
After his death (1545) the sculptor Alonso Berruguete executed his funerary
monument.

THEOTOKOPOULOS, JORGE MANUEL (1578-1631)

Son of El Greco and Doña Jerónima de las Cuevas, he was born in
Toledo in 1578 (this date is written in Greek characters on the slip of paper
held in the hand of the page-boy in *The Burial of Count Orgaz*). After 1603
the records of the Toledo archives make increasingly frequent mention
of him as assistant and factotum to his father. Working on his own account,
he painted the large altarpiece of Bayona de Titulcea (1609). After his
father's death he worked chiefly as an architect (completion of the Town
Hall of Toledo, 1613; funerary monument of Philip III, 1621; reconstruction of the Mozarabic Chapel of Toledo Cathedral, 1626). In 1621 he was
appointed building supervisor of the Municipality. He married three times.
His first wife, Alonsa de los Morales, gave him a son, Gabriel, born in 1605,

who took the cowl in 1622 under his mother's name, entering the Augustinian order. In 1621 he married Gregoria de Guzman who, after giving him three children, died in 1629. He married Isabel de Villegas in the following year. After a journey to Granada, he returned to Toledo, where he died on March 29, 1631.

THEOTOKOPOULOS, MANUSOS (1530-1604)

A mysterious relative, perhaps an elder brother, he was living with El Greco in 1603. Already in poor health then, he died in Toledo on December 13, 1604. His very existence had passed unnoticed until San Román's discoveries in the archives of Toledo. Several mentions of this name occur in 16th-century Venetian records. In 1572 one Manusso Theotocopoulos volunteered for service on a Venetian privateer being fitted out to harry Turkish commerce in the Mediterranean. El Greco's relative seems more likely to be the same man who, as a tax-collector in the Venetian administration at Candia from 1566 to 1583, was imprisoned for embezzling 6000 ducats, then freed in consideration of ill-health and allowed to journey abroad in search of means to make good his debt.

TRISTAN, LUIS (C. 1580-1624)

Luis Tristan (also called Luis de Escamilla, his mother's name) is, with Jorge Manuel, the only known disciple of El Greco, with whom he worked from at least 1603 to 1607. Dying relatively young in 1624, he nevertheless left a large number of works behind him. In them (for example *The Holy Trinity* in Seville Cathedral) we find the direct reflection of El Greco's figures and compositions, but considerably coarsened and thickened. In his best works—the Yepes Altarpiece (1616) and the Altarpiece of Santa Clara at Toledo (1620)—he combined the influence of El Greco with an increasingly pronounced variety of tenebrist realism that linked him up with the Valencian masters Ribalta and Ribera.

VALDIVIESO, JOSÉ DE (C. 1560-1638)

This Toledan priest, chaplain of the Mozarabic Chapel of the Cathedral, was one of the most popular Spanish religious poets of the early 17th century and enjoyed the friendship of Cervantes and Lope de Vega. Though he never attained their heights, he showed great skill and forcibleness in his use of the traditional forms and rhythms of the Spanish lyric. One of his best works is the *Romancero espiritual del Santísimo Sacramento* (Toledo 1612). Also a dramatic poet, he wrote some of the finest *autos sacramentales* of the day, for example the famous *Hospital de los Locos...*, a morality poem recently revived with much success in a stage version (first published in *Doce autos sacramentales y dos comedias divinas*, Toledo 1622).

SELECTED BIBLIOGRAPHY

The number of books and articles devoted to El Greco in recent times is so large that any attempt to choose among them becomes inevitably arbitrary to some extent. Our choice here has been governed by the desire to record (1) source works and catalogues of specialized exhibitions; (2) a select list of publications notable either for their contribution to our knowledge of El Greco or for the large number of reproductions they contain; (3) various brochures and magazine articles in different languages, most of them fairly recent, which may be of interest to the general reader and do not cover the same ground as the books listed here; and (4) for the additional interest they present, several specialized works on art and history indispensable for situating El Greco among the painters of his time and amid the various milieux in which he lived and worked. The titles under each heading are listed in chronological order.

In addition to the documentary material contained in Cossío's *El Greco* and in a few other works (such as ZARCO DEL VALLE, *Documentos de la Catedral de Toledo*, Centro de Estudios Historicos, Madrid 1916; P. ZARCO CUEVAS, *Pintores españoles*... and *Pintores italianos en San Lorenzo del Escorial*, Madrid 1932; BERNARDO GARCIA REY, *El dean D. Diego de Castilla y la reconstrucción de Santo Domingo el Antiguo*, Boletín de la Academia de Toledo, 1923), the standard source works are those of FRANCISCO DE BORJA DE SAN ROMÁN Y FERNÁNDEZ: *El Greco en Toledo*, Suarez, Madrid 1910, and *De la vida del Greco* (separate reprint in Archivo Español de Arte y Arqueología), 1927, which may be completed by shorter studies and articles on particular points of interest, as for example *El sepulcro de los Theotokopoulos*, 1912.
The chief texts of the older authors who wrote about El Greco may be found in F. J. SÁNCHEZ CANTÓN, *Fuentes literarias para la Historia del Arte español* (5 vols., Junta para Ampliación de Estudios and Consejo de Investigaciones Científicas, 1925-1941), as follows: Vols. I (SIGUENZA), II (MARTÍNEZ), III (PACHECO), IV (PALOMINO), V (various authors).

Source Works

Manuel B. Cossío, *El Greco*, 2 vols., Suarez, Madrid 1908. Standard work, of which two chapters, revised by the author, were subsequently published separately: *Lo que se sabe de la vida del Greco* and *El entierro del conde de Orgaz*, Suarez, Madrid 1914. Both were included in the reprint of the entire work (but with all illustrations, references and catalogues cut out) published in the Colección Austral, Espasa-Calpe, Buenos Aires 1944. — Maurice BARRÈS, *Greco ou le secret de Tolède*, Plon, Paris 1910; 2nd edition, supplemented, 1923. Still a standard work, in connection with which see P. GUINARD, *Barrès et le Greco*, Revue Hebdomadaire, Paris, July 1924. — J. F. WILLUMSEN, *La jeunesse du peintre El Greco*, 2 vols.,

Monographs

131

Crès, Paris 1927. — August MAYER, *El Greco*, Munich 1928. First icono-graphical catalogue, reproducing all the works ascribable to El Greco. — Jean CASSOU, *Le Greco*, Maîtres de l'art ancien, Rieder, Paris 1931. — Camille MAUCLAIR, *Greco*, Grands Artistes, Laurens, Paris 1931. — Eugène DABIT, *Les maîtres de la peinture espagnole : Greco, Velazquez*, Galli-mard, Paris 1935. — M. LEGENDRE and H. HARRIS, *Le Greco*, introduction et reproduction de l'œuvre, Hypérion, Paris 1937. — Christian ZERVOS, *Les Œuvres du Greco en Espagne*, Ed. Cahiers d'Art, Paris 1939. — Hugo KEHRER, *Greco als Gestalt des Manierismus*, Munich 1939. — Manuel GOMEZ MORENO, *El Greco*, Bibl. Arte Hispanico, Ed. Selectas, Barcelona 1943. — Id., *El Entierro del Conde de Orgaz, estudio critico*, Obras maestras del Arte Español I, Ed. Juventud, Barcelona 1943. — Jean BABELON, *El Greco*, Tisné, Paris 1946. — Marqués DE LOZOYA, *El San Mauricio del Greco, estudio critico*, Obras maestras del Arte Español VII, Ed. Juventud, Barcelona 1947. — Jean COCTEAU, *Greco*, Les demi-dieux, Paris 1947. — Ludwig GOLDSCHEIDER, *El Greco*, introduction and reproduction of his works, Phaidon, New York 1949 (2nd edition). — José CAMÓN AZNAR, *Dominico Greco*, 2 vols., Espasa-Calpe, Madrid 1950. Monumental work, strictly chronological, covering the life of El Greco and all works ascribed to him. — Antonina VALLENTIN, *El Greco*, Albin Michel, Paris 1954; English edition, Museum Press, London 1954. Biographical reconstitution based on a serious study of El Greco's works and period.

Chief
Magazine
Articles and
Shorter Studies

A. DE BERUETE, *El Greco, pintor de retratos*, Madrid 1914. — Emile BERTAUX, *Notes sur le Greco*, Revue d'art ancien et moderne, 1911-1913. — Conde DE CEDILLO, *De la religiosidad y del misticismo en las obras del Greco*, Boletín de la Sociedad Española de Excursiones, 1915. — José Ramón MELIDA, *El arte antiguo y el Greco*, Boletín de la Sociedad Española de Excursiones, 1915. — Lionello VENTURI, *La formación del estilo del Greco*, Boletín de la Sociedad Española de Excursiones, 1918. — Eugenio D'ORS, *Poussin y el Greco*, contained in *El nuevo glosario*, vol. V, Caro Raggio, Madrid 1922. — Elie LAMBERT, *Les procédés du Greco*, Gazette des Beaux-Arts, 1925. — Paul GUINARD, *Saint François dans l'œuvre de Greco*, Revue d'Histoire franciscaine, 1925. — Angel VEGUE Y GOLDONI, *En torno a la figura del Greco*, articles contained in *Temas de Arte y de Literatura*, Iris, Madrid 1928. — August L. MAYER, *The Greco : An Oriental Artist*, Art Bulletin, 1929. — E. WATERHOUSE, *El Greco's Italian Period*, Art Studies, 1930. — José CAMÓN AZNAR, *Bizancio y Italia en la obra del Greco*, Univer-sidad de Granada, 1944. — Natalia COSSIO DE JIMENEZ, *Notes on Greco's Birthplace, Education and Family...*, Oxford 1948. — Helmut HATZFELD, *Textos teresianos aplicados a la interpretación del Greco*, Clavileño, Madrid 1950. — G. FIOCCO, *Del Greco Veneziano*, Arte Veneta, 1951. — Bertina SUIDA, *El Greco y el arte italiano*, Archivo Español de Arte, 1951. — G. A. PROCOPIOU, *El Greco and Cretan Painting*, Burlington Magazine, 1952. — R. PALLUCCHINI, *Opere giovanili firmate e datate del Greco*, Arte

Veneta, 1952. — J. G. LEMOINE, *La luz en los cuadros del Greco*, Revista de Ideas Estéticas, 1954. — Ramón ROBRES, *El beato Ribera y El Greco*, Archivo Español de Arte, 1954.

Ricardo JORGE, *El Greco*, Universidad de Coimbra, 1913. — German BERITENS, *Aberraciones del Greco*, Fernando Fé, Madrid 1913. — Id., *El astigmatismo del Greco*, Madrid 1914. — Manuel MARQUEZ, *Sobre el supuesto astigmatismo del Greco*, Barcelona 1926. — Id., *Con Motivo del pretendido astigmatismo del Greco*, Madrid 1929. — Gregorio MARAÑON, *Nuevas notas médicas sobre la pintura del Greco*, Revista de las Españas, 1927. — Id., *El secreto del Greco*, in *Tiempo viejo y tiempo nuevo*, Madrid 1940. — Charles LALO, *La vision déformante de Greco*, Journal de Psychologie, 1932. — Arturo PERERA, *El porqué de la pintura del Greco*, Arte Español, 1953.

Pathological Studies

S. VINIEGRA, *Catálogo de la Exposición de obras del Greco*, Museo del Prado, Madrid 1902. — A. DE BERUETE and Conde DE CEDILLO, *Catálogo del Museo del Greco*, Madrid 1912. — SÁNCHEZ CANTÓN and VEGUE, *Nueva sala del Museo del Greco*, Madrid 1913. — Elisabeth DU GUÉ TRAPIER, *El Greco in the Collection of the Hispanic Society of America*, New York 1925. — *Catalogue de l'Exposition de Greco*, organized by the Gazette des Beaux-Arts, Paris 1937. On the paintings from the Royal Collection of Rumania, which formed the nucleus of this exhibition, see the article by A. BUSUIO-CEANU: *Les tableaux du Greco de la Collection royale de Roumanie*, Gazette des Beaux-Arts, 1934. — Catalogue of the exhibition *Le Greco: de la Crète à Tolède par Venise*, Galerie des Beaux-Arts, Bordeaux 1953 (with studies by Rodolfo PALLUCCHINI and Dr Gregorio MARAÑON).

Catalogues of Exhibitions and Museums

Marqués DE LOZOYA, *Historia del Arte hispanico*, vols. III-IV, Madrid 1940-1945. — August L. MAYER, *Historia de la pintura española*, 2nd edition, Madrid 1942. — Janine BATICLE, *Histoire de la peinture espagnole*, Tisné, Paris 1950. — Jacques LASSAIGNE, *Spanish Painting*, 2 vols., Skira, Geneva 1952. — Enrique LAFUENTE FERRARI, *Breve Historia de la Pintura española*, 4th edition, Madrid 1953. — Diego ANGULO INIGUEZ, *Pintura del siglo XVI*, Ars Hispaniae XII, Madrid 1955.

P. DE NOLHAC, *Les Collections de Fulvio Orsini*, Gazette des Beaux-Arts, 1884. — Id., *La Bibliothèque de Fulvio Orsini*, Paris 1887. — BRADLEY, *The Life and Works of Giulio Clovio*, London 1891. — Conde DE CEDILLO, *Toledo en el Siglo XVI*, Madrid 1901. — Giuseppe GEROLA, *Monumenti Veneti dell'Isola di Creta*, III, Venice 1908. — F. DE NAVENNE, *Rome, le Palais Farnèse et les Farnèses*, Albin Michel, Paris 1914. — Jean BABELON, *Jacopo da Trezzo et la construction de l'Escorial*, Bibl. Ecole des Hautes Etudes Hispaniques, Féret, Bordeaux 1929. — Louis BERTRAND, *Philippe II à l'Escorial*, Fayard, Paris 1929. — Sergio BETTINI, *La pittura di icone cretese, veneziana e i madonneri*, Padua 1933. — Werner WEISSBACH, *El Barocco como arte de la Contra-Reforma*, Madrid 1942.

General Works

INDEX OF NAMES

134

GAUGUIN Paul 116.
GAUTIER Théophile 115.
GÓNGORA Luis de 22, 33, 125;
Obras en Versos 34; *Fábula de Poli-femo y Galatea* 109, 125; *Soledades* 125.
GOURMONT Jean de 106.
GOYA Francisco de 30, 115.

GRECO El, Domenikos Theotoko-poulos, paintings:

Adoration of the Magi, Athens, Bena-kis Museum 50; *id.*, Copenhagen, Willumsen Coll. 50; *id.*, Rome, Borghese Gallery 50.
Adoration of the Name of Jesus (Dream of Philip II), Escorial 17, 21, 44, 92, 93.
Adoration of the Shepherds, Bergamo 14; *id.*, Madrid, Prado 32, 56; *id.*, Toledo, Santo Domingo el Antiguo 18; *id.*, formerly Coll. of the King of Rumania 26.
Annunciation, Bilbao Museum 97; *id.*, Budapest Museum 97; *id.*, Illescas, Hospital de la Caridad 97; *id.*, Madrid, Prado 97; *id.*, former-ly Coll. of the Marquis of Urquijo, Madrid 112; *id.*, Villanueva y Geltrú, Museo Balaguer 26, 97; *id.*, Zumaya, Museo de Zuloaga 97.
Apostolados, Almadrones (Guadala-jara) 80; *id.*, Madrid, Prado 80; *id.*, Oviedo, Coll. of the Marquis of San Félix 80; *id.*, Toledo, Cathe-dral 80; *id.*, Toledo, Museo del Greco 80.
Archbishop of Toledo, Escorial 79.
Assumption of the Virgin, Chicago, Art Institute 18, 56; *id.*, Toledo, San Vicente 30, 106, 107, 112.
Baptism of Christ, Madrid, Prado 24/26, 44.
Boy kindling a Flame, Naples, Pinaco-teca del Museo Nazionale 48, 50.

Burial of Count Orgaz, Toledo, Santo Tomé 8, 20, 23, 25, 30, 44, 60, 62, 64, 65, 79, 88, 90, 94/96, 121, 129.
Christ driving the Traders from the Temple, Boston, Museum of Fine Arts 100; *id.*, London, National Gallery 14; *id.*, Madrid, San Ginès 100; *id.*, Minneapolis, Insti-tute of Arts 14, 53, 54; *id.*, New York, Frick Coll. 100; *id.*, Rich-mond (Surrey), Cook Coll. 52.
Christ in the Garden of Olives, Buda-pest, formerly Herzog Coll. 100; *id.*, Lille Museum 100; *id.*, London, National Gallery 100; *id.*, Toledo (Ohio), Museum of Art 44, 46.
Christ on the Cross, Martín Muñoz de las Posadas, church 64; *id.*, Paris, Louvre 64, 85.
Coronation of the Virgin, Illescas, Hos-pital de la Caridad 102; *id.*, Madrid, Prado 102; *id.*, Talavera la Vieja, church 57, 102.
Crucifixion, Cincinnati, Art Museum 85; *id.*, Madrid, Prado 26, 85, 97, 98; *id.*, Toledo, San Vicente 85.
Descent from the Cross, Niarchos Coll. 56; *id.*, Venice, Private Coll. 14.
Dream of St Martin (miniature), Va-lencia, Colegio del Patriarca 96.
Espolio, Toledo Cathedral 7, 16, 18, 19, 40, 41, 43, 44, 47, 60; replicas 82.
Feast in the House of Simon, Chicago, Art Institute 44, 45, 100.
Healing of the Blind Man, Dresden, Gemäldegalerie 14, 52; *id.*, Parma, Galleria Nazionale 14, 52.
Holy Face, Madrid, Prado 42, 46.
Holy Family, Toledo, San Juan Bautista 33.
Immaculate Conception, Toledo, San Román 57.
Laocoön, Washington, National Gal-lery 102/106.

Portraits:

Vincentio Anastagi, New York, Frick Coll. 14.

Duke of Benavente, Bayonne, Musée Bonnat 70.

Jerónimo de Cevallos, Madrid, Prado 70, 71.

Giulio Clovio, Naples, Pinacoteca del Museo Nazionale 14, 49, 51.

Antonio Covarrubias, Paris, Louvre 70; *id.*, Toledo, Museo del Greco 70.

Diego Covarrubias, Toledo, Museo del Greco 70.

Alonso Ercilla y Zúñiga (?), Leningrad, Hermitage 70.

Dr Rodrigo de La Fuente, Madrid, Prado 70.

Pompeo Leoni (?), Glasgow, Stirling-Maxwell Coll. 70.

Cardinal Don Fernando Niño de Guevara, New York, Metropolitan Museum 66/69.

An Unknown Painter, Seville, Museo Provincial 70.

Fray Hortensio Félix de Paravicino, Boston, Museum of Fine Arts 70, 76, 77; *id.*, Madrid, Casa Torres Coll. 70.

Dr Pisa (miniature), Madrid, Dr Marañon Coll. 79.

Cardinal Gaspar de Quiroga, Munich, Private Coll. 66.

Captain Julian Romero, Madrid, Prado 90.

Presumed Self-Portrait, New York, Metropolitan Museum 30, 31.

Cardinal Tavera, Toledo, San Juan Bautista 66.

Rodrigo Vázquez, Madrid, Prado 70.

Portrait of a Man, Portrait of a Woman (miniatures), Valladolid, formerly Sobejano Coll. 74.

Woman with a Flower in her Hair, Glasgow, Stirling-Maxwell Coll. 66.

Woman with a Fur, Glasgow, Stirling-Maxwell Coll. 16, 115.

Studio Work: *The Family of Jorge Manuel*, Bryn-Athyn (Pa.), Pitcairn Coll. 28, 32.

Ascribed to El Greco: *Last Judgment*, Rhineland, Private Coll. 54, 93.

GRIMANI family 124.

GUZMAN Gregoria de 130.

HERRERA Juan 18, 124.

HOMER 40.

Illescas, Hospital de la Caridad 8, 29, 30, 64, 90, 97, 102.

ISARLO Georges 50.

JORGE MANUEL, see THEOTOKOPOULOS.

JORGE Ricardo 110.

JUSTI Carl 44.

KEHRER Hugo 50, 57.

LA FUENTE Dr Rodrigo de 70, 126.

LAMBERT Elie 111.

LA TOUR Georges de 115.

LEONARDO DA VINCI 122.

LEONI Pompeo 70.

Lepanto, Battle of 7, 15.

LONGHI Roberto 121.

LOUIS-PHILIPPE, King 115.

LULLY Jean-Baptiste 59.

Madrid 7, 8, 13, 22, 73, 125, 127; Colegio de Doña María de Aragón 8, 26; San Ginès 100; Alcázar 125; Museo Cerralbo 88; Prado 18, 26, 32, 44, 46, 56, 57, 66, 73, 78, 80, 85, 96, 102, 112, 116.

MALLARMÉ Stéphane 125.

MANCINI Giulio Cesare 15, 121.

MANET Edouard 115.

THE COLORPLATES

CONTENTS

THIS VOLUME

THE FIFTEENTH OF THE COLLECTION

THE TASTE OF OUR TIME

WAS PRINTED

BOTH TEXT AND COLORPLATES

BY THE

SKIRA

COLOR STUDIO

AT IMPRIMERIES RÉUNIES S.A., LAUSANNE

FINISHED THE FIFTEENTH DAY OF FEBRUARY

NINETEEN HUNDRED AND FIFTY-SIX

*The plates were engraved by Guezelle et Renouard, Paris
except for those on pages 42, 71, 87, engraved by Wetter, Zurich
and those on pages 19, 24, 27, 41, 55, 61, 81, 84, 94, 95, 98, 99, 107, 117
engraved by Schwitter S.A., Basel*

*Photographs by Hans Hinz, Basel
(pages 3, 17, 19, 20, 23, 24, 27, 28, 41, 42, 55, 61, 62, 63, 65, 71, 72, 74, 75,
81, 83, 84, 87, 89, 92, 94, 95, 98, 99, 107, 108, 117, and dustjacket)
by Henry B. Beville (pages 31, 32, 45, 53, 58, 67, 68, 69, 77, 103, 104, 105, 114)
by Arte e Colore, Milan (pages 12, 38)
by Claudio Emmer, Milan (pages 48, 51)
Photograph on page 102 obligingly lent by The National Gallery of Art,
Washington, D.C.*

PRINTED IN SWITZERLAND